Valorie -
Believing you
are healed & restored!

XO
Nicole

HI GOD

(IT'S ME AGAIN)

HI GOD
(IT'S ME AGAIN)

Nicole Crank

Fedd Books
P.O. Box 341973
Austin, TX 78734
www.thefeddagency.com

Published in association with The Fedd Agency, Inc., a literary agency.

Scripture quotations marked ESV are from the ESV® Bible (The Holy Bible, English Standard Version®), copyright © 2001 by Crossway, a publishing ministry of Good News Publishers. Used by permission. All rights reserved.)

Scripture quotations marked NIV are from the New International Version®, NIV®. Copyright © 1973, 1978, 1984, 2011 by Biblica, Inc.™ Used by permission of Zondervan. All rights reserved worldwide. www.zondervan.com The "NIV" and "New International Version" are trademarks registered in the United States Patent and Trademark Office by Biblica, Inc.™

Scripture quotations marked NASB are taken from the NEW AMERICAN STANDARD BIBLE®, Copyright © 1960, 1962,1963,1968,1971,1972,1973,1975,1977,1995 by The Lockman Foundation. Used by permission.

Scripture quotations marked KJV are from The Authorized (King James) Version. Rights in the Authorized Version in the United Kingdom are vested in the Crown. Reproduced by permission of the Crown's patentee, Cambridge University Press.

Scripture quotations marked NKJV are taken from the New King James Version®. Copyright © 1982 by Thomas Nelson. Used by permission. All rights reserved.

Scripture quotations marked MSG are taken from THE MESSAGE, copyright © 1993, 1994, 1995, 1996, 2000, 2001, 2002 by Eugene H. Peterson. Used by permission of NavPress. All rights reserved. Represented by Tyndale House Publishers, Inc.

Scripture quotations taken from the Amplified® Bible (AMP), Copyright © 2015 by The Lockman Foundation. Used by permission. www.Lockman.org.

Scripture quotations taken from the Amplified® Bible Classic Edition (AMPC), Copyright © 1954, 1958, 1962, 1964, 1965, 1987 by The Lockman Foundation. Used by permission. www.Lockman.org.

Scripture quotations marked HCSB are taken from the Holman Christian Standard Bible®, Used by Permission HCSB ©1999, 2000, 2002 ,2003, 2009 Holman Bible Publishers. Holman Christian Standard Bible®, Holman CSB®, and HCSB® are federally registered trademarks of Holman Bible Publishers.

Scripture quotations marked ISV taken from the Holy Bible: International Standard Version®. Copyright © 1996-forever by The ISV Foundation. ALL RIGHTS RESERVED INTERNATIONALLY. Used by permission.

Scripture quotations marked (CEV) are from the Contemporary English Version. Copyright © 1991, 1992, 1995 by American Bible Society. Used by permission.

Paperback ISBN: 978-1-943217-57-1
Hardback ISBN: 978-1-943217-60-1
eISBN: 978-1-943217-58-8

Printed in the United States of America

First Edition 15 14 13 10 09 / 10 9 8 7 6 5 4 3 2

TABLE OF
CONTENTS

INTRODUCTION

Tell me if this is your story, too. No matter how early you set the alarm, it seems like you could use more time to make everything happen.

Brew the coffee, wake the kids, handle the dog, do the dishes, laundry, oh yeah . . . I'm supposed to wear clothes—ugh! What to wear . . . would people notice if I wore the same thing as a couple days ago? Text, phone . . . *I need that list* . . . where is my phone? Food. No time for food . . . what?! I'm already supposed to be gone. Let's GO! *Where are my keys?!*

Most of us don't take the time to make a home-cooked breakfast. Really, a granola bar and coffee are considered a luxury. And that's just about what we do or don't feed our stomachs. Sometimes we go hungry—not out of neglect, but out of distraction. We have so many things pulling for our attention that nothing actually *gets* our attention.

That happens to our spiritual feedings too. (Don't tune me out because you think I'm about to make you feel guilty! This is a no-guilt zone ☺.) We run around so frantically trying to get things done that we don't actually stop and *do* anything spiritual. We are "spiritual" but not spending time with the Spirit.

This is why I wrote this book. To help you—oh mercy, to help *me*—in those moments when our spirit needs strength and encouragement. When we need help with our relationships or with our jobs or in our finances. When the phone rings, and a friend wants us to help solve their problems. When we read a post on Facebook, Instagram, or Snapchat that is begging for advice, but we're too consumed with our own lives to help. We know we should go to God, but how can we find the time? And once we get with him, what do we even *say*?

I have a "Confessions" CD that I had no idea would be as popular as it was. It's not a tell-all of my past (thank goodness!); it's verses and affirmations that believers can confess over their lives. You just pop it in, and I read you a Scripture or positive affirmation to say over your life. Then, I give you a moment to say the verse or affirmation back. The CD exploded!

I think this CD was popular for three reasons:

- People didn't have to worry about what to pray. I essentially told them.
- The affirmations were short, simple, powerful, and to-the-point. They were accessible for your busy lives.

- God's Word is powerful and true! Sometimes we worry so much about what to say when God has already given us some pretty awesome words in his Word.

Because I love this CD, and I love free stuff, I want to give you the CD. If you go to nicolecrank.com/confessions, you can download the mp3 for *free*. I think it will jumpstart you on your journey through this devotional and help you be more comfortable talking to God and boldly and confidently confessing his promises over your life.

This book is written encouragement for you, right now. It's for those clutch situations and urgent scenarios—those everyday, "somebody-please-tell-me-I'm-OK-and-I'm-going-to-make-it" moments.

The devotionals are God's Word to you. They're simple, straightforward, and give you words when you may not have any or may not have the time to *think* of any. And—like the "Confessions" CD—these devotionals speak to everyday topics and thoughts that are likely on your mind. Worry . . . doubt . . . money . . . stress . . . health . . . Sound familiar?

These are bite-size pieces, written as prayers, that you have time for every day. There is no pressure to read a whole chapter—each devotional is super short. (If you're a parent or in a busy office, the bathroom is a good place to keep this book. Sometimes I go in there and shut the door for a couple minutes even when I don't have to use the bathroom just to breathe!) The devotionals will give you a chance to do three things:

1. Express the struggles to God
2. Remember who God is and declare his promises to you
3. Ask God for help in specific ways and affirm his power in the trouble

These devotionals will make sure you eat spiritually on a regular basis and, over time, give you bigger, stronger faith in the midst of your busy life.

One of the greatest parts about this book is that it's packed with Scripture. I included a few Bible verses at the end of each devotional (told you I was making it convenient!), and God's Word is paraphrased in my words in just about every message. What I'd love is for you to read these prayers and verses out loud to yourself several times and see which ones pop out to you. Could God maybe be trying to tell you something?

The power of God's Word is amazing! Try letting these words and verses soak into your heart and mind, and feel life flow back into you.

I MISS YOU, GOD

Hi God. Why do I have to fight so hard to get a few minutes alone with you?

It's like the universe knows that I'm finally sitting down for time with you, and it starts to fight me. The phone rings, someone knocks at the door, the dryer buzzes, the kids yell… and on and on and on.

Then I feel guilty—like maybe I'm being selfish for carving out this time alone with you. I almost feel like I should be doing more to help my family, friends, work, or other people I love.

Why is it that trying to spend time with you can be such a battle?

Wait a minute . . .

The enemy sees how I gather strength when I'm with you. He sees that peace comes to me when I spend time talking to you and reading your Word. He knows I become sharper in my mind and spirit after being with the King of Kings. That's why it's so hard! The enemy knows that if I get with you, I will be refueled and refreshed. He knows he'll lose, and I'll win!

I can't let myself be fooled into thinking there is only incentive in working at my job or being with people. There is unbelievable reward in simply spending time with you!

- You graciously provide me with knowledge I don't have, answers I need, and wisdom beyond what I could ever get on my own.
- I get direction on which way to go and what decision to make, favor I don't deserve, and forgiveness I can't earn.
- You pour out rest in my soul and blessing beyond my wildest dreams and imagination!

God, I want you in my life so badly. I'll fight for time reading, praying, seeking, and asking. Thank you for always meeting me where I am.

God's Word

"He who dwells in the shelter of the Most High
will remain secure and rest in the shadow of
the Almighty [whose power no
enemy can withstand]."
— Psalm 91:1 AMP

"But when you pray, go into your room, close
the door and pray to your Father, who is unseen.
Then your Father, who sees what is done in
secret, will reward you."
— Matthew 6:6 NIV

"But his delight is in the law of the LORD,
And in his law he meditates day and night.
He shall be like a tree
Planted by the rivers of water,
That brings forth its fruit in its season,
Whose leaf also shall not wither;
And whatever he does shall prosper."
— Psalm 1:2-3 NKJV

HOW DO I FIND PEACE?

Hi God. Sometimes when I feel a tightness in my chest and find myself sighing, I know my peace is gone. It's funny how other people notice it even before I do. They'll ask, "What's wrong?"

Why does that happen?

I guess I know I'm not at peace because I'm worried, anxious, or fidgety. It's hard to be at peace and get a headache at the same time. (That should be a big indicator to me!)

How do I find peace in a crazy, noisy world? The news is literally yelling about how bad the world is, people in traffic are road-raging for no reason, and at the store, people are more likely to growl than to smile. Yikes, we really need you.

When my heart is at war, when my emotions run high, and when I'm nervous and can't sit still, I can't possibly think clearly and make the best decisions. I can't get my peace from this world. I have to get it from you.

Peace tells me the right way to go. It's what I'm supposed to follow. I should be led with peace. It's how I know whether I'm going the right way or making a decision I'll regret later.

Peace is so important—no peace, no go. If I have peace, I'll go. People ask me, "Why did you decide to do that?" and I'll tell them it's because I had peace about it. The peace of God.

I get peace by keeping my mind on you. When I think about everything I have to get done today and start to get overwhelmed, I will reach out to you, God. Help me do this! Give me peace! When I call on you, it seems like I can breathe you in, and then I have inner calm. Just the sound of those words soothes my soul.

Right now, I purposefully and intentionally make my life different from all the people running at a crazy, stress-filled pace. I choose to operate in your strength and peace.

God, I call on you. I lean into you. Let your peace rest in me.

God's Word

"You will keep him in perfect peace,
whose mind is stayed on You,
because he trusts in You."
— Isaiah 26:3 ESV

"Peace I leave with you; my peace I give you. I
do not give to you as the world gives. Do not let
your hearts be troubled and do not be afraid."
— John 14:27 NIV

"Let the peace of Christ [the inner calm of one
who walks daily with Him] be the controlling
factor in your hearts [deciding and settling
questions that arise]. To this peace indeed
you were called as members in one body [of
believers]. And be thankful [to God always]."
— Colossians 3:15 AMP

"And the peace of God [that peace which
reassures the heart, that peace] which tran-
scends all understanding, [that peace which]
stands guard over your hearts and your minds
in Christ Jesus [is yours]."
— Philippians 4:7 AMP

• • ● ● ● • •

I WILL ASK

Hi God. Why is it that I hesitate to come straight to you whenever I need something? You'd think I'd have stopped going around this mountain by now.

Instead, I keep trying to figure out things on my own. I'm staying up at night and losing sleep thinking about things! That's not what you want for me. You want me to rest and relax in you. I'm ready to sleep!

You say that I don't have what I need because I don't *ask* you for it. Asking you should be the first thing I do, not my last resort. That sounds so simple!

Sometimes I feel bad about asking, though—like I'm being selfish or begging. Other times, I think I'm too lazy, or I just forget. Not anymore! If I'm not asking for your favor, blessing, and increase, then I'm not exercising my faith.

Even though some things seem impossible, and I don't see how they could possibly happen, *it's not my job* to make them happen. All you ask me to do is believe in you. I'm the believer, and you're the performer. Miracles are your expertise, and you're just waiting for me to ask so that you can move.

The Bible tells me to ask for *anything* and for everything. I'm told to ask you, Father, *in Jesus' name,* and you will do it for me. Not just because you love *Jesus* so much, but also because you love *me* just the same. That's awesome!

I know that as soon as I ask, you are faithful to start moving, arranging, speaking, orchestrating, and coordinating on my behalf. It's exciting to know that you're so busy at work for me. All I have to do is *ask!*

And finally, you say that when I pray *in faith* I'm to believe that I receive it . . . *even before it shows up!* So I'll believe, right now, that I've already got it.

Look out, Father! I'm not going to be so shy anymore. I'm going to start *asking* you for a lot more things.

Thank you. It'll be *fun* to have you more involved in every step of my day!

God's Word

"You lust and do not have. You murder and covet and cannot obtain. You fight and war. Yet you do not have because you do not ask."
— James 4:2 NKJV

"And in that day you will ask Me nothing. Most assuredly, I say to you, whatever you ask the Father in My name He will give you. Until now you have asked for nothing in My name; ask and you will receive, so that your joy may be made full."
— John 16:23-24 NKJV

"If you abide in me, and my words abide in you, ask whatever you wish, and it will be done for you."
— John 15:7 ESV

MY GREATEST ASSET

Hi God. Attitude is such a little thing that makes a *big* difference. My good attitude puts me in the place of greatest potential and opportunity.

What happens to me is only 10 percent of my life. But 90 percent is how I *choose* to react. Today, when I walk into a situation where everything is going wrong, I won't cave in to my emotions. I will take them captive and manage them. I know the right attitude will set the right atmosphere.

My positive attitude is one of my *greatest assets*. It will draw people to me—it's contagious! When people get around me, they'll suddenly start feeling better. I'm excited to breed love and light wherever I go.

The world does a good job telling everyone what they are not. God, I will let you use me to tell your people who they *are*. They are loved by you. They are valued by you. They are wanted by you. Your peace, your joy, your love, and your blessing will pour out of me. Please flow through me to pour life and motivation into others.

No matter how much I lift up those around me, I know I can always do it more. Please open doors of opportunity for me to forge new friendships and relationships so that I can build up more and more people.

Seeing the good is what you created me to do, and it's ultimately up to me to choose the attitude that I want. Today, I choose to go with *you*!

God's Word

"The one who searches for what is good finds favor,, but if someone looks for trouble, it will come to him."
— Proverbs 11:27 HCSB

"Love bears all things [regardless of what comes], believes all things [looking for the best in each one], hopes all things [remaining steadfast during difficult times], endures all things [without weakening]."
— 1 Corinthians 13:7 AMP

"But David strengthened himself in the LORD his God."
— 1 Samuel 30:6 ESV

THE BEST VERSION OF ME

Hi God. I'd really like to improve myself. I want to move on. I want to move up. I want to quit messing up. I want to be *better*.

I've tried moving forward, but to be honest, I've tried doing it all on my own. My way, with sheer willpower, doesn't work.

So how do I make my life better?

Your Word says to trust you to lead my life. Honestly, I kind of hate hearing that because I like being in control. But if your way leads me to a better life of blessing, happiness, and peace, then I guess I need to get over having to be in control and start following your instructions.

The good news is, I'm not alone in this. You're in me, and you're greater than my current circumstances or anything that comes along next. I know you live on the inside of me and want me to listen so that you can show me how to become better. And not just a little better . . . you want to help me become great!

You make up for my shortcomings, and you magnify my strengths. Your favor makes me look better than I could ever imagine and opens doors for me that I don't deserve. You make me better than I could ever be on my own.

When I actually listen to what you tell me and obey the words you give me, you make me the best version of me. When I do things your way, you make me everything I'm not.

I don't have to try to be better. I've been chasing the wrong dog. I should be chasing *you*!

God's Word

"And if you faithfully obey the voice of the Lord your God, being careful to do all his commandments that I command you today, the Lord your God will set you high above all the nations of the earth. And all these blessings shall come upon you and overtake you, if you obey the voice of the Lord your God."
— Deuteronomy 28:1-2 ESV

"You are of God, little children, and have overcome them, because He who is in you is greater than he who is in the world."
— 1 John 4:4 NKJV

"And in Him you have been made complete, and He is the head over all rule and authority."
— Colossians 2:10 NASB

"If you are willing and obedient, you shall eat the good of the land."
— Isaiah 1:19 ESV

THIS IS BIG

Hi God. I know that a swordless David faced off with a nine-foot giant named Goliath. I read about how an entire sea split right down the middle so that a bunch of Hebrew slaves could escape. And I remember the story where Daniel was thrown into the lion's den. Instead of being eaten, he was brought out safely the next day and promoted.

But I'm not some hero from the Bible. I'm just me. And what I'm facing is really big. Too big for me. I know that you major in miracles, so this is so easy for you. But it is huge for me. I can't handle something of this size!

Help me to remember that nothing is bigger than you, God. What I see as a mountain, you see as an opportunity to prove your power. You not only *move* the mountain, but you also pulverize it into particles so small they just blow away like dust.

- No problem is bigger than you are.
- No enemy is wiser than you are.

- No sickness can out-maneuver you.
- No addiction can withstand your awesome anointing.
- No deficiency in me can slow you down.

The *impossible* is not even a challenge for you. You're beyond this realm I'm stuck in. You are greater than what I can imagine. Bigger. Stronger. Smarter. Faster. Better. Wiser. Your grace overflows, and your mercy abounds. Your love never ends. You never give up, and you certainly never fail.

I give you, God, what looks like a giant to me. It's in your hands now, and I'm excited to see what you do with it!

"You are the God who performs miracles;
you display your power among the peoples."
— Psalm 77:14 NIV

"Yours, O LORD, is the greatness and the power
and the glory and the victory and the majesty,
indeed everything that is in the heavens and the
earth; Yours is the dominion, O LORD, and You
exalt Yourself as head over all."
— 1 Chronicles 29:11 NASB

"LORD, the God of our ancestors, are you not
the God who is in heaven? You rule over all the
kingdoms of the nations. Power and might are
in your hand, and no one can withstand you."
— 2 Chronicles 20:6 NIV

"I am the LORD, the God of all mankind. Is
anything too hard for me?"
— Jeremiah 32:27 NIV

LIVING STRONG

Hi God. I feel like I'm waging a war against my own flesh. If I had my way, I'd just lie on the couch all day and eat ice cream!

I want to start making healthier food choices, drinking more water, and getting outside to walk more. But my crazy flesh just wants everything to eat right now, and I don't want to exercise!

I know that when I resist the urge to fill up on junk food and soda, I always feel so much better about myself. I know I don't want to end up suffering.

- I don't want all the health problems I see around me.
- I don't want to depend on alcohol or drugs as a crutch to get through the day.
- I don't want to wear my body out and then have to pray for replacement parts.

I want to live long and strong on this earth and serve you! Will you help me, God?

The Bible says that my mouth is satisfied with good things, and my youth is renewed like the eagle. I love the word *satisfied*. I'm calling satisfaction being able to walk on two strong legs all the days of my life. Sleeping like a baby and waking up renewed. Living with a strong heart and lungs that beat well and breathe easy.

I claim that I'll spend my years with joints that bend and move easily and free of pain. I declare I will always look, act, and feel ten years younger than I am in Jesus' name. I am craving and eating healthy foods that sustain me.

You've given me the Holy Spirit as my own personal spiritual trainer inside of me. With you, all this is possible. You are ready to help me make good choices if I'll just pause for a second and ask.

God, you know me intimately. You know my weaknesses and the things that consistently trip me up. Show me how to overcome these temptations, set aside any extra baggage, and walk in your divine health.

With your help, I'm going to make healthier decisions so I live a long and strong life!

God's Word

"Bless the Lord, O my soul,
And forget not all His benefits:
Who forgives all your iniquities,
Who heals all your diseases,
Who redeems your life from destruction,
Who crowns you with lovingkindness
and tender mercies.
Who satisfies your mouth with good things,
So that your youth is renewed like the eagle's."
— Psalm 103:2-5 NKJV

"With long life will I satisfy him,
and show him my salvation."
— Psalm 91:16 NKJV

"Beloved, I pray that you may prosper in all things
and be in health, just as your soul prospers."
— 3 John 2 NKJV

LITTLE FOXES

Hi God. I feel like I need to change my life in a big way. But it's kind of overwhelming to think about changing everything all at once. Where do I start?

Your Word says that "little foxes" can spoil the entire big vineyard. In other words, some things look like enormous problems, but really, just making a few small adjustments can make a tremendous difference. Just a few little corrections? I think I can handle that!

Surely, with you, the great and mighty God living inside me, I can do little changes. Inch by inch, it'll be a cinch!

- I'll have a little more faith.
- I'll love a little more easily.
- I'll forgive the little debt because you forgave my big debt.
- I'll allow a little patience to work in me.
- I'll follow your leading and be obedient to your Word, one day at a time.

What am I afraid of? A little work? A little challenge? Giving you a little trust? I won't let these little tweaks keep me from the big peaks you have for me! I'm not where I want to be yet, but I'm not where I used to be either.

I'm excited, God, that you're helping me make these small adjustments. I'm going to live a big life and not allow the little foxes to slow me down!

God's Word

"Catch for us the foxes, the little foxes that ruin the vineyards, our vineyards that are in bloom."
— Song of Solomon 2:15 NIV

"But let patience have its perfect work, that you may be perfect and complete, lacking nothing."
— James 1:4 NKJV

"If you are faithful in little things, you will be faithful in large ones. But if you are dishonest in little things, you won't be honest with greater responsibilities."
— Luke 16:10 NLT

"He said to them, 'Because of your little faith. For truly, I say to you, if you have faith like a grain of mustard seed, you will say to this mountain, "Move from here to there," and it will move, and nothing will be impossible for you.'"
— Matthew 17:20 ESV

I AM BLESSED

Hi God. Whether I realize it at the moment or not, you have blessed me in ways I can't even grasp. Your Word says that the windows of heaven are open, and you are pouring out blessings for me I can't contain. I say, "Let it rain!"

The commanded blessing in the Bible tells me that if I live a life that honors you and obey your Word, then blessings will chase me down and overtake me. It says I will be blessed in the city and blessed in the country. I will be blessed going in and blessed going out.

I thank you that I am blessed in my health, my family, and my finances. I thank you that I am blessed in my moods, my attitudes, and my emotions. I am blessed in my job and given rare opportunities, favor, raises, and promotions.

I thank you that I am blessed with friendships and relationships beyond my expectations. I thank you that I am blessed with your favor and that doors of opportunity open for me. Everywhere my feet go, I am blessed!

I thank you, Father, that I enjoy the best in every area of my life. I have the blessing of Abraham, Isaac, Jacob, and Jesus. I am blessed when I don't even *feel* like I am blessed. I am like a tree planted by the rivers of water. Everything I do prospers.

Help me remember that I am blessed so that I can be a blessing to others. I am thankful that you bless me so that I can continue to bless you and others.

Your Word says that when I give, you give back to me. But you don't merely give back—you give back with *bonus* and *blessing*. You are causing all grace and all favor to come to me in abundance.

The more I bless others, the more I find myself blessed. Your goodness, your love, your kindness just keeps coming back to me! Your Word declares that my giving increases the fruits of my righteousness.

I am blessed to be a blessing!

God's Word

"I will make you a great nation;
I will bless you
And make your name great;
And you shall be a blessing."
— Genesis 12:2 NKJV

"So let each one give as he purposes in his
heart, not grudgingly or of necessity; for God
loves a cheerful giver."
— 2 Corinthians 9:7 NKJV

"You will be enriched in every way so that
you can be generous on every occasion, and
through us your generosity will result in
thanksgiving to God."
— 2 Corinthians 9:11 NIV

"Give, and it will be given to you: good
measure, pressed down, shaken together, and
running over will be put into your bosom. For
with the same measure that you use, it will be
measured back to you."
— Luke 6:38 NKJV

MY GOOD REPORT

Hi God. Sometimes I feel like I'm *stuck* in my own thoughts—as if, somehow, I have to learn to think differently.

I often catch myself dwelling on my past—how I've messed up and even what other people say about me. All these thoughts are like a broken record in my head playing over and over again.

I know you didn't create me to think on this low level. I have to clear my head to be able to fill it with your thoughts. I'm your child. I should think like you!

So right now, God, I purpose in my heart to think like you. Your Word says that I'm renewed, made strong, and built up by thinking what you tell me to think—that I'm actually *changed* when I think what you desire.

So, what *do* you tell me to think about? You say to think about the good stuff. Things that are true. What's true from you?

- It's true that you are for me and not against me.
- It's true that you love me more than I can know.
- It's true that you've forgiven me for everything

I've ever done.
- It's true that your mercy goes past any sin I will ever commit.

I recall things that are honest, just, and pure—the positive and the possible. I bring to mind things that are lovely and of good report. You gave me another day on this planet. You've drawn me closer to you. You're moving in my life.

As a man thinks, so he is. When I concentrate, intentionally, on the good, I can feel my mood changing, worry leaving, excitement and expectation coming, hope rising, and faith building on the inside of me.

My good report is:

- The sunset was beautiful.
- You gave me another day on this planet to work things out and allow you to work in my life.
- You've drawn me closer to you—I can tell that because we're talking right now!
- You're moving in my life. Even if I can't see it yet, I know it's true.

What do you know, God? This really works! I think I'm on the right track. I feel the way I feel because I think the way I think!

I'm feeling better already because I'm thinking like you!

God's Word

"'For My thoughts are not your thoughts,
Nor are your ways My ways,' says the LORD.
'For as the heavens are higher than the earth,
So are My ways higher than your ways,
And My thoughts than your thoughts.'"
— Isaiah 55:8-9 NKJV

"And do not be conformed to this world, but be transformed by the renewing of your mind, that you may prove what is that good and acceptable and perfect will of God."
— Romans 12:2 NKJV

"Finally, brethren, whatever things are true, whatever things are noble, whatever things are just, whatever things are pure, whatever things are lovely, whatever things are of good report, if there is any virtue and if there is anything praiseworthy—meditate on these things."
— Philippians 4:8 NKJV

"For 'who has known the mind of the LORD that he may instruct Him?' But we have the mind of Christ."
— 1 Corinthians 2:16 NKJV

I CHOOSE YOU

Hi God. Sometimes I don't *feel* like I have a choice because I'm just mad or sad . . . or I feel completely helpless! I have to admit, though: even when I think I don't have a choice, I actually *am* choosing. I'm choosing to forfeit my choice.

I might not have control over my circumstances, but I do have the power to decide how I'm going to *react* in my circumstances. But if I don't intentionally choose to believe that you're working on my behalf, then that's not really faith. That, probably, won't please you and may even short-circuit my miracle.

My mouth can be a deep, dark well of defeat or a refreshing spring of life. It all depends on how I *choose* to use it. I guess that's why you tell me to choose life on purpose—because it won't happen any other way.

Death and life are in the power of my tongue, so I need to *choose* life—especially when it's so tempting to just gripe about my situation instead of believing you for the best.

If I don't stand in faith, who will stand in faith for

me? I need to continually think "faith thoughts" and speak "faith words."

So I guess it's pretty simple. Either I believe in you and your Word, or I don't.

My attitude is a choice. My joy is a choice. Persistence is a choice. Faith is a choice. Trusting you is my choice. I choose you!

God's Word

"But without faith it is impossible to please Him, for he who comes to God must believe that He is, and that He is a rewarder of those who diligently seek Him."
— Hebrews 11:6 NKJV

"The mouth of the righteous is a well of life, But violence covers the mouth of the wicked."
— Proverbs 10:11 NKJV

"I call heaven and earth as witnesses today against you, that I have set before you life and death, blessing and cursing; therefore choose life, that both you and your descendants may live."
— Deuteronomy 30:19 NKJV

"Fight the good fight of faith, lay hold on eternal life, to which you were also called and have confessed the good confession in the presence of many witnesses."
— 1 Timothy 6:12 NKJV

I WANT TO COMPLAIN RIGHT NOW

Hi God. I'm sorry, but I guess I have a talent for pointing out what's wrong with any situation. Sometimes it seems like there is Crisco on my tongue, and negative things just slip right out before I even notice the words I use.

That's not my intent. It isn't even what I want to focus on. And I sure don't want to be that person who people don't want to be around because I act like a "Debbie Downer." I'm really going to need your help with this! I know complaining can hold me back in this world and with you.

In the wilderness, the Israelites had so much blessing, but they couldn't even see it. They were out of slavery, the Red Sea parted, and manna (fast food) was falling down—right out of the clear blue sky. They never even had to cook! Their clothes didn't wear out. You even gave them quail for meat when they asked for it and water in the middle of the desert. But they still complained, and it kept them from the blessings you had for them.

I know my grumbling can hold me back in this world and with you. When I complain about my blessed life, it certainly doesn't compel you to act.

I don't want my future blessing to be hijacked because I'm not acknowledging the good in my present situation. I don't want to stay here on this level for the rest of my life.

My attitude, my praise, and my thanks to you shouldn't be based on my circumstances. That just limits you to only what I can see. But I want to unleash you into the realm of what I *can't* see.

Thank you, God, for loving me without fail! Thank you that I woke up today, and your mercies were new. Thank you that every day you load me down with the awesome benefits of being your child.

God's Word

"And the people complained in the hearing of the Lord about their misfortunes, and when the Lord heard it, his anger was kindled, and the fire of the Lord burned among them and consumed some outlying parts of the camp."
— Numbers 11:1 ESV

"Give thanks in all circumstances, for this is God's will for you in Christ Jesus."
— 1 Thessalonians 5:18 NIV

"Bless the LORD, O my soul, and forget not all his benefits."
— Psalm 103:2 ESV

WHO AM I?

Hi God. The world tries to tell me that my future has already been decided by my past—where I was born, where I went to school, what I've done, and even what was done to me. People make it sound like what happened in the past is unchangeable.

Here's the thing: That might be their experience, but they obviously don't know you at all. You don't think the way we think or work the way we work. In fact, I'm not any of those things that have played back in my mind so many times:

- I am not what my parents say.
- I am not how my spouse sees me.
- I am not what the people at work think about me.

It doesn't matter if what others say about me is "fact" or not. Your truth is bigger than their fact. I am who *you* say I am!

You say I am *redeemed*, *forgiven*, *accepted*, and *made*

righteous in Christ. And I know that the truth you say is way bigger than anything man could ever say about me.

You have relieved me of the shame of my past. I don't have to feel unworthy. I'm your child—a masterpiece created for good works.

I won't spend my life looking in a rearview mirror. My past is just that: *past.* It's over, gone, erased forever. I'll spend my life looking forward to the marvelous things you have in store for me.

What was done to me, I could not control, but you work all things together for my good. You've gone out before me to light my path, lead my way, and show me which way to go.

Thank you, Lord, that my future looks good and bright and blessed!

"And the people complained in the hearing of the Lord about their misfortunes, and when the Lord heard it, his anger was kindled, and the fire of the Lord burned among them and consumed some outlying parts of the camp."
— Numbers 11:1 ESV

"Give thanks in all circumstances, for this is God's will for you in Christ Jesus."
— 1 Thessalonians 5:18 NIV

"Bless the LORD, O my soul, and forget not all his benefits."
— Psalm 103:2 ESV

I DON'T KNOW
WHAT TO SAY

Hi God. There are times when I just don't know what to say.

I want to yell and be mad. I want to grumble about how unfair life is and what's bugging me. I want to say how hard things are. I want to say that I'm tired and not happy. I want to complain and tell everybody what's happening to me. But you say not to let that stuff creep out of my mouth. You want me to focus on the promise. You want me to concentrate on you.

OK, that's a big adjustment.

So what, exactly, *should* I say?

I will talk about the time you brought me unexpected money when I needed it most. I'll remember the time you healed me of my headache, my cold, my backache, and so much more. I'll say *out loud to the universe* how good you've been to me. I'll tell how you saved me. How you redeemed me. How you keep lifting me up even after I fail and fall short time and time again.

Your Word tells me to speak to the mountain in the

name of Jesus, so I'll say to the problem, "Get out of my way! I refuse to allow you any power over my life. That is my God's place!"

That's what I'm doing right now. I'm not scared to approach you with your promises.

I'm testifying out loud to your goodness in my life. You supply every need and even the desires of my heart.

- I desire health! You will satisfy me with long life.
- I desire peace! Peace is a gift you have given me.
- I desire blessing! Your blessing makes me rich, and there is no sadness in it.

I know what to say now. I will no longer give my words to the enemy, to negativity, or to my problems. You're the One with power. You are my Father, my God, and I trust in you!

God's Word

"Let no corrupt communication proceed out of
your mouth, but that which is good to the use
of edifying, that it may minister grace
unto the hearers."
— Ephesians 4:29 KJV

"Truly, I say to you, whoever says to this mountain, 'Be taken up and thrown into the sea,' and
does not doubt in his heart, but believes that
what he says will come to pass, it will be done
for him. Therefore I tell you, whatever you ask
in prayer, believe that you have received it, and
it will be yours."
— Mark 11:23-24 ESV

"Death and life are in the power of the tongue,
And those who love it will eat its fruit."
— Proverbs 18:21 NKJV

I WON'T QUIT

Hi God. The enemy will try to get me to give up when I am closest to my breakthrough. That's when he's at risk of losing, so I won't quit!

I may get knocked down, but I'm not out. Even when I'm hurt, I'm still here.

It doesn't matter how I got hurt or the type of attack against me. It doesn't matter whether a friend did me wrong, my business is slow, I've been cheated, or I'm sick. The fact is, I. Am. Still. Here.

I've made up my mind to stay in the fight. The battle isn't mine anyway. The battle is yours, and the victory is mine!

I can't quit. I'm blessed beyond any curse. Your promise never ends. Your joy is the strength I need when I don't have strength of my own. You fill in my gaps. Where I leave off, your might and power are just *beginning*!

When my breakthrough is close, the enemy will try whatever he can to distract, derail, or make me wave the white flag in defeat. I will *not* quit, though. If I receive bad news, I'll take it as the enemy is scared.

If there was no fight, the Bible would have never told me to put on the whole armor of God. That means I wear you. You encompass me. You protect me. You have me covered from the top of my head—with the helmet of salvation—to the bottom of my feet . . . my shoes of peace. I like those shoes.

You are my sword and my shield. You *equip* me for anything and *empower* me through everything. You defend and protect me.

If you prepare me—and you have—if you give me strength—and you do—if you fight for me—and you will, as you have promised, *why* would I ever quit? You are always with me. *I will not quit.* I am on my way to victory.

God's Word

"We are hard-pressed on every side, yet not crushed; we are perplexed, but not in despair; persecuted, but not forsaken; struck down, but not destroyed."
— 2 Corinthians 4:8-9 NKJV

"Thus says the Lord to you: 'Do not be afraid nor dismayed because of this great multitude, for the battle is not yours, but God's.'"
— 2 Chronicles 20:15 NKJV

"Therefore put on the full armor of God, so that when the day of evil comes, you may be able to stand your ground, and after you have done everything, to stand. Stand firm then, with the belt of truth buckled around your waist, with the breastplate of righteousness in place, and with your feet fitted with the readiness that comes from the gospel of peace. In addition to all this, take up the shield of faith, with which you can extinguish all the flaming arrows of the evil one. Take the helmet of salvation and the sword of the Spirit, which is the word of God."
— Ephesians 6:13-17 NIV

NO DOUBT

Hi God. I know I'm in trouble when a friend tries to tell me to look at the bright side or cheer me up, and I roll my eyes because I only see the downside.

Doubt doesn't get me anywhere. It certainly never leads to winning. Doubt never invented anything or took on new territory. It never brings out the best in people or even the hero in me. Doubt is a tool of the enemy.

If the enemy can get me to question your goodness— why I was created, the gifting you gave me, or who I am in you—then he can derail me from my future. If I let him plant a seed of doubt in my mind, then he has a hope of succeeding.

That's what happened to Eve in the garden. The serpent mentioned the thought, "Can it really be? God just wants to keep good things from you" in her mind. Liar! Seeds of doubt, left unchecked, lead to a fall.

Satan even tried it several times with Jesus! "If you are the Son God . . ." He was trying to get Jesus to hesitate about who he was. "If" is the devil's badge of doubt. If he tried to get Jesus to doubt who *he* was, then he's going to try to get me to doubt who I am, too.

Doubt is a well-worn page from the enemy's playbook.

God, you don't want disbelief clouding the doorstep of my heart or casting a shadow on what I know you can do. You want no hesitation and no fear of asking. When I pray and ask in faith, I believe you go to work *immediately* to make things happen!

I am a believer, not a doubter. I ask in faith, and you bring it to pass. You're better than I can even imagine. You're bigger than I can comprehend. Your grace extends beyond the borders of my knowingness, and your mercy is so expansive, I will never be able to understand it.

So God, I will ask in faith. No doubting. Right now, I ask you for . . .

Healing in my body & mind
Finish school (A)(home)
Get a good Job (50,000)
Money in Savings (20,000)

God's Word

"I will answer them before they even call to me.
While they are still talking about their needs,
I will go ahead and answer their prayers."
— Isaiah 65:24 NLT

"But let him ask in faith, with no doubting, for
he who doubts is like a wave of the sea driven
and tossed by the wind. For let not that man
suppose that he will receive anything from the
Lord; he is a double-minded man, unstable in
all his ways."
— James 1:6-8 NKJV

"For assuredly, I say to you, whoever says to this
mountain, 'Be removed and be cast into the sea,'
and does not doubt in his heart, but believes that
those things he says will be done, he will have
whatever he says. Therefore I say to you, whatever things you ask when you pray, believe that
you receive them, and you will have them."
— Mark 11:23-24 NKJV

LAUGHTER,
NOT WORRY

Hi God. I have to admit that I'm sitting here worrying about something that hasn't even happened yet. I guess it's possible that it won't *ever* happen. But I keep thinking, *What if it does?*

I know it sounds silly, but I just can't stop running every possible scenario through my head. And yet, I still don't feel better, and I'm not any better off than I was when I started.

That's not how you want me. You don't want me depressed and letting the news and challenges of today get the best of me.

I'm trying really hard not to let negative thoughts rule my day because I don't want the enemy to win. No way! I am *not* on his team. I am a child of the Most High God!

You're my strength and my redeemer, God, so I'm speaking to these stupid worries, stressful thoughts, and anxious scenarios and telling them that *nothing* is too big for you.

You know it all and sit in heaven and laugh. You're not laughing at me; you're laughing at the ridiculousness that is trying to pull me down: the news of the hour, layoffs, the economy, health reports, what my loved ones are up to, what my haters are trying to do. While I've been worrying, you laugh.

If you're laughing, I should be laughing, too! You're bigger than any problem, greater than any emergency, and in control of the entire universe for all of eternity. I know you've got this.

A cheerful heart does good—like medicine. Help me, Father, to cast all my cares on you so I can laugh . . . right along with you!

God's Word

"He who sits in the heavens shall laugh;
The Lord shall hold them in derision."
— Psalm 2:4 NKJV

"A merry heart does good, like medicine,
But a broken spirit dries the bones."
— Proverbs 17:22 NKJV

"Cast all your anxiety on him because
he cares for you."
— 1 Peter 5:7 NIV

"For God has not given us a spirit of fear, but
of power and of love and of a sound mind."
— 2 Timothy 1:7 NKJV

I CRY OUT TO YOU

Hi God. I like to think I'm tough. Tough *enough*, anyway.

But sometimes, things get to be too much. I let gossip and people's "chit chat" get to me, or I start to feel betrayed and abandoned. And then, the next thing you know, my eyes well up, and I can't help but cry.

The problem is that I never really feel any better afterwards. Nothing has changed. I need help with this.

I know, I don't have to be strong by myself. Your promise says that when my heart is broken—when I feel crushed, and I cry out to you—that you'll save me from everything that's hurting me. When I crumble, I can always ask for help, and you'll *run* to my side. When I invite you into my hurt, you bring hope.

I need hope because it protects me from depression and self-pity. Hope makes it possible for me to get my mind off of me and my ability to try to fix things, and instead, puts my focus on you.

Hope. Hope in you will keep me from falling apart. As I hold onto hope and faith, the weight of my problems comes off me and transfers to you. It feels so good to be able to breathe!

From now on, I'll give you all my troubles because I know you can handle them. You are the God of hope. Putting my confidence in you brings me peace and happiness, and I'll trade crying in the bathroom for peace and happiness any day!

Now my time isn't wasted. It's productive. You make me strong, dry all my tears, and restore my soul. With you on my side, who or what can mess with me?

I promise, Lord—no more crying about the problem. I'm too busy crying out to *you* and watching your grace go to work for me!

God's Word

"Yes, my soul, find rest in God;
my hope comes from him."
— Psalm 62:5 NIV

"Now may the God of hope fill you with all joy
and peace in believing, that you may abound in
hope by the power of the Holy Spirit."
— Romans 15:13 NKJV

"When the righteous cry for help, the LORD hears
and delivers them out of all their troubles.
The LORD is near to the brokenhearted
and saves the crushed in spirit."
— Psalm 34:17-18 ESV

"The poor man cried, and the LORD heard him
And saved him out of all his troubles."
— Psalm 34:6 NKJV

ENEMY WHO?

Hi God. When someone's "talking trash" about me, when money is tight, when my problems seem like an enormous tidal wave . . . racing toward me with a force so overwhelming that it keeps me awake at night . . . I have to remember what you promised me.

You didn't say that trouble wouldn't come my way or that I wouldn't have an enemy. You assured me that I would never have to stand on my own and that you'd hold me up with your righteous hands. You have gone out before me, *made a way for me*, and made a trap for my enemy.

I know there will always be people out there who want to cause me trouble and hurt me. But you already have plans to take whatever junk they throw at me and use it for my own good. My enemy sees impending defeat, but you see a new way to bless me that I wasn't expecting.

Right now, I say in faith:

- I am a child of God, and my enemy does not

get to touch me.

- Evil's principalities and powers are bound from operating against me in any way.
- When problems come in, like a flood, the standard of the Lord is raised up against them.
- The God of victory is on my side. The blood of Jesus has been applied.

You are my rock. You are my defense.

My enemy can't move me because he would have to go through you first. I don't have to hide. You have my back, and peace is headed my way when trouble tries to rear its ugly head. You, God, are coming to dismantle, distract, derail, deactivate, and destroy all of my enemies.

God, please surround me and protect me from every evil thing. I don't have to hide because you have my back. When enemies come against me, they don't stand a chance with the God of all heaven and earth on my side. I'm not only a winner—I'm also more than a conqueror!

God's Word

"Fear not, for I am with you;
Be not dismayed, for I am your God.
I will strengthen you,
Yes, I will help you,
I will uphold you with My righteous right
hand."
— Isaiah 41:10 NKJV

"Yet in all these things we are more than
conquerors through Him who loved us."
— Romans 8:37 NKJV

"When a man's ways please the Lord,
He makes even his enemies to be at
peace with him."
— Proverbs 16:7 NKJV

"For the Lord your God is He who goes with
you, to fight for you against your enemies, to
save you."
— Deuteronomy 20:4 NKJV

STEPPING OUT

Hi God. You want me to have faith because without faith it's impossible to please you. It takes faith to do anything I can't do on my own. If I could do it all by myself, I would never need faith.

What is faith?

- Faith is trusting in you—trusting that you'll lift me up when I can't hold myself up.
- Faith is trusting that you'll fill in the gaps when I come up short.
- Faith is trusting your promises and knowing that you meant those promises for *me*.

Faith in you doesn't even begin until I am out beyond myself. It must have been so scary for Peter to step out of a safe boat onto the dark and stormy water.

If I rely on my natural sight, I'll never be able to step out of my boat and walk on water. When the situation around me is rocky, and I can't see how to make things happen, *that* is when you demand my faith.

If I want to accomplish amazing things no one has ever done, then I have to step out of the boat—out of my safety zone—and believe! You make the impossible, *possible.*

My faith begins where my ability ends. I put my life in your hands.

Today, I'm stepping out!

"But without faith it is impossible to
please Him, for he who comes to God must
believe that He is, and that He is a rewarder of
those who diligently seek Him."
— Hebrews 11:6 NKJV

"Now faith is the substance of things hoped for,
the evidence of things not seen."
— Hebrews 11:1 NKJV

"For we walk by faith, not by sight."
— 2 Corinthians 5:7 NKJV

"But Jesus looked at them and said, 'With
men it is impossible, but not with God; for with
God all things are possible.'"
— Mark 10:27 NKJV

HURRY UP!

Hi God. There are times when I get frustrated and think that you're not going fast enough. I want you to move faster. Bring my blessing sooner. Open a new door earlier. Heal me right now. Bring the money today!

I'm not where I want to be yet. I want to be there already—like last year! *Why don't you come help me?*

Even though I'm not where I want to be, I have to admit, I'm definitely not where I *used* to be. You've brought me up. You've changed me. You've transformed my life. I'm thankful, God. I just want to be farther . . . faster.

At the same time, when I look at the size, the scope, and the entirety of my dream, it scares me a little bit. It's so much bigger than I am. If I focus on my dream as a whole, I don't think I can master it.

How can I want your blessing to get here even faster but be overwhelmed by it all at the same time?

You say a new season is beginning in my life—a season I've never experienced before.

Little by little, you say you can help me, so I can

handle it. Gradually, you'll create and reveal solutions to me and give me patience to wait for more to come. You'll guide me one step at a time so that I have time to increase, adjust, and handle the success. You'll support me so that once I "take the land," I can stay in it.

This pace that sometimes frustrates me was created to sustain me. It's a plan I can keep up with so that I win for a lifetime and not only for a moment.

You are the author and the finisher. You don't want me to start and not finish or to taste success and blessing and then lose it. You want me to live in your land of promise.

Step by step, I can do this with you!

God's Word

"Make me walk along the path of
your commands,
for that is where my happiness is found."
— Psalm 119:35 NLT

"I will instruct you and teach you in the way
you should go;
I will counsel you with my eye upon you."
— Psalm 32:8 ESV

"Wealth gained hastily will dwindle,
but whoever gathers little by little
will increase it."
— Proverbs 13:11 ESV

BEING ME

Hi God. I know you created me this way *on* purpose, *for* a purpose!

Even though I might not like everything about myself, I know you made me this way for a reason. You molded me in your image. Wow! Just like when people look at my parents and then look at me and know we're related, I look that much like you. That's why I can't be unhappy about the way you made me.

You, the Master Creator, made me. Not "poor little ol' me" . . . *me*. I am *your* child—your masterpiece created in Christ Jesus. Not only am I fully accepted by you, I'm also manufactured, fashioned, and *designed* by you! You thought so much of me when you made me that you allowed Jesus to be crucified to save me. I guess that means you think I'm "to die for."

When I question why you made me different and unique, when I wonder why I'm not like everyone else, I remember that it's because you made me special. I am one of a kind. Those distinctive and one-of-a-kind things about me are the things that set me apart.

You don't make junk. You make beautiful things out of the dust of the earth and breathe your life into them—into *me*! You made me the way you *want* me, and if you like me this way, I should like me too. You even say I am wonderfully made.

You not only intentionally crafted me this way, you also *called* me by my name. You didn't have some random person or obscure life in mind. You had *me* in mind—in all my unusual and interesting ways. You had me, my name, and my *life* in your mind.

For me, being "me" is authentic, organic, and on-purpose. There is only one person in all of history with my thumbprint—a thumbprint as distinct as the imprint you intend for me to leave on this earth. I am the only "me" ever created, and no one can be a better "me" than *me*.

God's Word

"So God created man in His own image; in
the image of God He created him; male and
female He created them."
— Genesis 1:27 NKJV

"I will praise You, for I am fearful-
ly and wonderfully made;
Marvelous are Your works,
And that my soul knows very well."
— Psalm 139:14 NKJV

"Before I formed you in the womb I knew you;
Before you were born I sanctified you;
I ordained you a prophet to the nations."
— Jeremiah 1:5 NKJV

FEAR NOT

Hi God. Why not? Why not fear? Everybody else is afraid. Everything on the news is bad. The economy is struggling. People are being killed. Leaders are corrupt. And they're even calling for rain. The news makes me not even want to leave the house!

The Bible says that men's hearts fail them because of fear. I'm only human, and it sounds like there might be good reasons to be afraid.

So, why not fear?

The phrase "do not be afraid" is written 365 times in the Bible. God, it's like you're reminding me every single day to live fearlessly! I don't have to give in to fear, no matter what's happening around me.

I declare that no plague, terrorism, economy lapse, or craziness can threaten me because you are with me. You strengthen me and even hold me up when I feel like I can't stand on my own.

Fear and faith have something in common: they both ask me to believe in something I can't see. So I choose to believe in you. I will believe in you more than

I believe in the things that scare me.

You didn't create me to be afraid. I should not fear if I have the God-of-the-Angel-Armies on my side! You gave me your Spirit, power, and soundness on the inside. And when I feel like I don't have the strength, and I can't make it, you give me your power. Talk about a supercharge!

Miracles happen when I put more energy in the dreams you have given me than in my fears. You custom-designed my future. If I don't accomplish my dreams and what you have for me, who will?

Life is not about fearing; it's about fulfilling. I will do it, even if I am afraid.

God's Word

"Fear not, for I am with you;
Be not dismayed, for I am your God.
I will strengthen you,
Yes, I will help you,
I will uphold you with My
righteous right hand."
— Isaiah 41:10 NKJV

"Yea, though I walk through the valley of the
shadow of death,
I will fear no evil;
For You are with me;
Your rod and Your staff, they comfort me."
— Psalm 23:4 NKJV

"For God has not given us a spirit of fear, but
of power and of love and of a sound mind."
—2 Timothy 1:7 NKJV

"Do not, therefore, fling away your fearless
confidence, for it carries a glorious
and great reward."
— Hebrews 10:35 AMP

MORE THAN ENOUGH

Hi God. When I look at my checking account balance, and then I look at what I need, sometimes the two don't add up.

This isn't a new problem. You've heard it all before and solved the same problem a million times. Bringing bread, money, and harvest to your children is easy for you.

When Abraham was climbing up one side of a mountain with his son as his only available sacrifice, he was walking in faith that you would provide for him. While they were climbing one side, you had a ram of provision climbing up the other. And rams don't even climb that high on mountains! God, you provide even in *impossible* circumstances.

You don't do for one person what you wouldn't do for another. So what you did for Abraham, I'm asking you to do for me. I believe that you, God, will supply all my needs according to your riches.

You promise that I will always have sufficiency in all things.

- sufficient funds for my housing
- necessary money for education
- sufficient savings for vacation
- sufficiency in generosity
- enough funds to start the endeavor you are calling me to
- sufficient funds to increase
- adequate money to feed not only my own family, but other families too

But you are not a God who is just sufficient. You are a more-than-enough God!

I'm a tither and a generous giver, and you make promises to people who do what I do. When I'm generous to you, it comes back to me so many times more than what I gave.

You promise to open the windows of heaven and pour out blessings—blessings so big I can't contain them. You did that to the widow with the container of oil, God. You blessed her to the limits so that she couldn't contain it.

God, I'm making room to contain more blessing!

God's Word

"And my God will liberally supply (fill until full) your every need according to His riches in glory in Christ Jesus."
— Philippians 4:19 AMP

"And God is able to make all grace [every favor and earthly blessing] come in abundance to you, so that you may always [under all circumstances, regardless of the need] have complete sufficiency in everything [being completely self-sufficient in Him], and have an abundance for every good work and act of charity."
— 2 Corinthians 9:8 AMP

"'Bring all the tithes into the storehouse,
That there may be food in My house,
And try Me now in this,'
Says the Lord of hosts,
'If I will not open for you the windows of heaven
And pour out for you such blessing
That there will not be room enough
to receive it.'"
— Malachi 3:10 NKJV

IT HURTS TO FORGIVE

Hi God. I've been hurt so deeply in my life. Sometimes thoughts, faces, smells, and places bring up a pain I thought was gone.

I try to forget what happened, but then something comes up and reminds me of it all over again. Old words and feelings come pouring in, leaving me feeling like part of me is broken, and another part is bitter. I want to cry and fight back, all at the same time.

No wonder you said we have to forgive the same person not seven times, but seventy times seven. Sometimes that's how many times I think about the same hurt!

I feel like if I let my pain go, then my betrayer is getting away scot-free! Somehow, I'm holding the offense to try to make them pay. After all, they're living life as if everything is just fine, and it's not!

But I'm the one hurting and unhappy because unforgiveness doesn't hurt my enemy—it only hurts me. It's like I'm drinking poison and waiting for someone else to die.

I need your help, God, to forgive, to release, to let it go. This is my opportunity to break the chain that is binding me to my pain so that I can go where I am trying to go without getting stuck in my past.

Forgiveness is an act of faith. It's trusting that you are a better justice-maker than I am. Father, I release my desire to get even and leave all issues in your capable hands.

I know that you are a just, fair, and merciful God. That's one reason I love you. I just had to come to another level of faith and trust in you to give you this. I choose to forgive all those who have wronged me in any way, and I have peace in my mind.

I'm done drinking poison. I'm over being labeled the victim. I'm finished dragging this hurt around and around. I choose to live in freedom.

Today, I set the prisoner free . . . because that prisoner is me!

"Then Peter came to Him and asked, 'Lord,
how many times will my brother sin against
me and I forgive him and let it go? Up to seven
times?' Jesus answered him, 'I say to you, not
up to seven times, but seventy times seven.'"
— Matthew 18:21-22 AMP

"If you forgive anyone anything, I too forgive
[that one]; and what I have forgiven, if I have
forgiven anything, has been for your sake in
the presence of [and with the approval of]
Christ, to keep Satan from taking advantage of
us; for we are not ignorant of his schemes."
— 2 Corinthians 2:10-11 AMP

"And do not give the devil an opportunity
[to lead you into sin by holding a grudge, or
nurturing anger, or harboring resentment, or
cultivating bitterness]."
— Ephesians 4:27 AMP

IN NEED OF COMPANIONSHIP

Hi God. I'm lonely.

I feel like I've been singled out. I don't like being on the outside looking in, but I'm not sure I fit in anywhere. I would love to have some close friends who I could talk to—friends who wouldn't judge me.

I guess everyone wants to be needed and needs to be wanted. That's your plan for my life, God. You created me for relationship.

From the beginning of time, your intent was for me to touch other people—to love them and speak encouragement into their lives in ways no one else will be able to. You have destined people who not only *want* me in their lives, but also who *need* me in their lives.

If I sow this into other people's lives, I will reap strong relationships in my own.

When I see someone who needs a friend, I'll try to love them like Jesus would. I will sow seeds of attention, favor, friendship, and encouragement into their lives, believing that you'll sow that back into mine in abundance! I'll be the kind of friend to others that I want in my life.

There's someone out there—right now—looking for a friend like me. I know that you're leading me to that relationship. I'll foster strong friendships that will take me toward my destiny and not away from it.

Good friends are precious gifts from heaven. I will not take for granted the abundance of godly, encouraging people you have sent into my life.

I decree and declare that the favor of God is on my life. People will look at me and like me. People are attracted to me because the light of God shines out of me and draws people to me.

I thank you, in advance, for the many blessed relationships you are sending in my direction. I'll honor them, but not put them before you. You are my closest friend and my most intimate confidant. I hold that place in my life for you.

"Two are better than one, because they have a good return for their labor. If they stumble, the first will lift up his friend—but woe to anyone who is alone when he falls and there is no one to help him get up."
— Ecclesiastes 4:9-10 ISV

"As iron sharpens iron, so a friend sharpens a friend."
— Proverbs 27:17 NLT

"One who has unreliable friends soon comes to ruin, but there is a friend who sticks closer than a brother."
— Proverbs 18:24 NIV

A NEW NAME

Hi God. Help me to see myself with your eyes!

Paul said, "I look through a glass darkly." Sometimes that's the way I feel. I really can't see things as clearly as you do.

I want to please you so badly, but then I mess up. I get mad. I blow it. I do something dumb, and I just want to kick myself. It feels like I take no steps forward, but then, three steps back.

But that's not what you see. What you see and what I see are different. You look at my heart. You know me so much better than I even know myself. You see the best in me.

You see the best in all people.

- When a man called Simon denied you, you saw a rock and called him Peter.
- In Saul, a mass murderer of Christians, you saw Paul, the writer of two-thirds of the New Testament.
- In Jacob, a slippery used-car-salesman-type

trickster, you saw a man you called "triumphant with God" and named him Israel.

You saw such great things in these people that no one else could see. And then, you gave them all a new name!

I need to adopt your names for me. In your Word you call me victor, blessed, overcomer, chosen, holy . . . even *royal* and *masterpiece*. Wow. That's big stuff—especially when I don't always feel like a winner or priceless treasure.

You see me in these ways, and *you call me by these names*. Even if I'm a little shy about believing everything you have called me to be, I can latch on to the fact that *you* believe I can be those things. I know your Word doesn't come back to you without accomplishing what you sent it for.

I'll say it out loud right now: I'm a victor! I'm blessed! I'm an overcomer! I am holy and chosen! I am royal and a masterpiece created by my Father who loves to do great things. I see it now. Thank you, God.

God's Word

"But the Lord said to Samuel, 'Do not consider his appearance or his height, for I have rejected him. The Lord does not look at the things people look at. People look at the outward appearance, but the Lord looks at the heart.'"
— 1 Samuel 16:7 NIV

"But you are a chosen generation, a royal priesthood, a holy nation, His own special people, that you may proclaim the praises of Him who called you out of darkness into His marvelous light."
— 1 Peter 2:9 NKJV

"So shall My word be that goes forth
from My mouth;
It shall not return to Me void,
But it shall accomplish what I please,
And it shall prosper in the thing for
which I sent it."
Isaiah 55:11 NKJV

I WANT TO
BE HAPPY

Hi God. There are times when I'm fine. I'm content. I feel happy. But then some ding-a-ling comes along and "road rages" me for no reason. Or I get someone incredibly rude at the store. Or a co-worker is in a totally foul mood and just ruins my day.

Poof. Happiness gone!

Your Word says, "count it all joy." I haven't been counting it all joy. In fact, sometimes, I've been counting the whole day as a loss. I had happiness for a minute, but I let someone hijack it.

I guess my joy isn't too hard to steal if all it takes is someone in a bad mood. I shouldn't be letting people pull me down with them. Instead, I should be helping them up.

The enemy is a thief! (You warned me about that.) So when I'm happy, he's going to try to spoil it. When I'm walking in love and your blessing, he's going to try and rip them off.

I have been letting the enemy rip off my "happy"

way too easily. I haven't been just allowing the enemy in—I've been holding the door wide open! It's almost like I've been saying, "Here you go, crabby people—just take my cheer away!" Nope. Not anymore.

I'm closing the door on the joy stealers. I'm dead-bolting that puppy and guarding my happiness and my peace like it's something precious . . . because it is!

Joy isn't what happens to me; it is what happens *through* me!

I'll count whatever happens joy because I know the plan of the enemy was at work, and today he loses! Blessed are those who learn to praise you and rejoice no matter what.

God's Word

"Count it all joy, my brothers, when you meet trials of various kinds, for you know that the testing of your faith produces steadfastness."
— James 1:2-3 ESV

"The thief comes only to steal and kill and destroy. I came that they may have life and have it abundantly."
— John 10:10 ESV

"Blessed are the people who know
the joyful sound!
They walk, O Lord, in the light of
Your countenance.
In Your name they rejoice all day long,
And in Your righteousness they are exalted."
— Psalm 89:15-16 NKJV

"Happy is he who has the God of Jacob
for his help,
Whose hope is in the Lord his God."
— Psalm 146:5 NKJV

WHAT'S GOOD ABOUT ME?

Hi God. When I look at this huge world, I find myself wondering if my small life makes any difference at all. I don't feel significant in the grand scheme of things. I don't know that I really stand out in any specific area.

I'm alive and moving, but not good at anything in particular. So is there more for me? I'm sure the enemy would love for me to get stuck here, discouraged and doubting myself. But I won't let that happen. I have to put my mind, my thoughts, and my focus on you.

You actually knew me before I was even born. You thought about me. You took time creating me in an exact and well-thought-out way. You intentionally gave me certain personality traits. You formed me to thrive and feel more alive doing specific things. You made me naturally good at certain things I might not even notice because they come so easily to me.

These traits aren't trivial; they're purposeful.

You created me to flourish using the gifts and talents you put in me—traits I might not even value yet. The abilities you gave me, they are irrevocable. No one can take them away. The only one who can hinder them is me by not tuning into them and using them. I might have done that before, but not anymore!

Today, I take time to think about those things I naturally do well. And God, I'm going to figure out how to use those things for you. God, open doors of opportunity and reveal to me my deeper purpose.

I vow that I will listen to and lean into you. I will tune into your voice, and I will live and fulfill the intended purpose you designed me for. Your future for me is great!

Thank you for making me special.

God's Word

"I chose you before I formed you in the womb;
I set you apart before you were born.
I appointed you a prophet to the nations."
—Jeremiah 1:5 HCSB

"For you created my inmost being;
you knit me together in my mother's womb.
I praise you because I am fearfully and
wonderfully made;
your works are wonderful,
I know that full well."
— Psalm 139:13-14 NIV

"For the gifts and the calling of God are
irrevocable [for He does not withdraw what He
has given, nor does He change His mind about
those to whom He gives His grace or to whom
He sends His call]."
— Romans 11:29 AMP

HEAL ME!

Hi God. I need healing in my body. You say in the Bible that you are the Lord who heals.

I believe that you are a healer, but sometimes I'm not sure I qualify. I feel like I don't deserve to be healed because I'm just not good enough.

But healing isn't something I can earn. It's a gift from you. It's free. It's your mercy and grace, not my works or righteousness. It's received by faith, like salvation. I believe that you saved me, so I can also believe that you will heal me. It's not about if I'm worthy; it's about my faith in you and your goodness.

You heal me because *you* are good, not because *I* am good. In the gospels, person after person asked Jesus to heal them, and every time he said, "I am willing." Your Word says you will heal *all*. And I am a part of all!

I'll confess what your Word says concerning my body and healing—not what happened to a friend, not what Google says, or even what a well-meaning doctor says. I'll confess what *you* say.

So according to your Word and instruction, I

confess with boldness, with confidence, with faith in you right now:

- Sickness and pain have no place in my body.
- Every disease and virus that touches my body dies instantly.
- Every organ, every cell, every tissue, every joint, and every system in my body functions in perfection—in the name of Jesus!
- By his stripes, I am healed—from the top of my head to the soles of my feet.
- Jesus died for my sickness, so I don't have to live with it.

Thank you for healing me, Father!

"When evening had come, they brought to Him many who were demon-possessed. And He cast out the spirits with a word, and healed all who were sick, that it might be fulfilled which was spoken by Isaiah the prophet, saying: 'He Himself took our infirmities and bore our sicknesses.'"
— Matthew 8:16-17 NKJV

"Surely he took up our pain and bore our suffering, yet we considered him punished by God, stricken by him, and afflicted. But he was pierced for our transgressions, he was crushed for our iniquities; the punishment that brought us peace was on him, and by his wounds we are healed."
— Isaiah 53:4-5 NIV

"God anointed Jesus of Nazareth with the Holy Spirit and with power, who went about doing good and healing all who were oppressed by the devil, for God was with Him."
— Acts 10:38, NKJV

• • ● ● ● • •

WHEN PEOPLE
HURT ME

Hi God. It hurts so badly to pour my love and energy into someone, and then, get nothing in return. I really thought we were close. I still love them, but obviously, the love only goes one way.

I'm tempted to stop putting myself out there for new relationships. I'm afraid it's not worth it. I feel like building a big wall around my heart to keep people out.

Part of me wants to talk about the people who hurt me and tell others how they've mistreated me. Their love for me failed, so why can't I talk about how wrong they did me? But that's not what you would do. Your love *never* fails.

I want to say, "an eye for an eye." But you say to turn the other cheek. You want me to sow forgiveness into others so that I can be forgiven by you and them. Ugh! So what now?

Now, I give forgiveness to people who I don't want to forgive, and you forgive me. Now, I walk in love toward those who aren't acting lovely to me, and you show me love unconditional. Now, I keep my mouth shut about how others have done me wrong, and you shut the mouths of my enemies.

You really know how to motivate someone!

I'll act like my Father. I will follow your example. When I extend grace to people who have hurt me, you bless me in the area where I need it most. And right now, I need grace in the area of strong relationships.

Thank you, God, for healing my heart and meeting all my needs, including my relationships. Thank you for providing me with strength to get over my hurt feelings. Thank you, God, for taking such good care of me.

I believe that you have people seeking me out, right now, for precious friendships and long-lasting relationships—for fun and love and good times and laughs.

I believe there are wonderful people, praying right now, to meet someone just like me!

God's Word

"But I say to you, Do not resist the one who is evil. But if anyone slaps you on the right cheek, turn to him the other also."
— Matthew 5:39 ESV

"And whenever you stand praying, forgive, if you have anything against anyone, so that your Father also who is in heaven may forgive you your trespasses."
— Mark 11:25 ESV

"Bearing with one another, and forgiving one another, if anyone has a complaint against another; even as Christ forgave you, so you also must do."
— Colossians 3:13 NKJV

WHAT I DO MATTERS

Hi God. Sometimes I work and work and wonder if anything I do even matters anyway. The world moves so fast, and it's so big. And I want to make a difference—I really do. But some days it seems like I'm doing good even just to remember where I am and where I'm supposed to be going.

Sometimes negative thoughts come at me so fast it's like they smack me upside the head. It makes me wonder why I'm even here.

I hear other people talk about fulfilling their purpose or being called to complete a task. I'm not sure what my purpose is because, in the grand scheme of things, I'm not sure how much "I" really matter.

That's why your words mean so much. Thank you for writing them down so I can be reminded that you made me on purpose. I needed to hear that from you so badly!

I might not fully realize why you wanted or needed me, but before I was born you had a plan for me. You knew how I'd turn out. You, God, King of Kings and Lord of Lords, took time to create *me*! And you only do things that matter!

You spent your valuable time thinking exactly how you would construct me—just the way I am, right here, in this city, at this job, with my exact personality, and gifted in my own quirky way. (I say quirky; you say *masterpiece*.)

You planned me for this moment in time. You've got something extraordinary in mind. Nothing you do is random. There's a specific reason for me being here—a divine destiny. In your eyes, I'm special!

You know the end from the beginning. Everything you do is on purpose, so that means I was created on purpose. I was planned. Intended. Needed. Significant. Important. You wanted me, and that's never changed.

God, that means I really do matter. Your purpose lives inside of me. Show me your perfect plan!

God's Word

"Before I formed you in the womb I knew you
[and approved of you as My chosen instrument],
And before you were born I consecrated you [to
Myself as My own];
I have appointed you as a prophet to the nations."
— Jeremiah 1:5 AMP

"Just as [in His love] He chose us in Christ
[actually selected us for Himself as His own]
before the foundation of the world, so that we
would be holy [that is, consecrated, set apart
for Him, purpose-driven] and
blameless in His sight."
— Ephesians 1:4 AMP

"But you are a chosen generation, a royal
priesthood, a holy nation, His own special
people, that you may proclaim the praises of
Him who called you out of darkness into His
marvelous light."
— 1 Peter 2:9 NKJV

I FEEL UNLOVED

Hi God. Sometimes I feel so far away from everyone, including you. I don't blame people if they wouldn't want to be around me. I just don't feel like I'm living up to my part of the bargain.

I get mad, fly off the handle, and then spout off my big mouth. Sometimes I lie (just a little), thinking it doesn't hurt anybody. But when I think about it later, I can't take it back. The damage is done, and I hear in my head, *Fail.*

Then I think to myself, *How could anyone love someone like me?*

Even with you. I try to do what I think will make you happy, but then I get busy. I stop reading my devotional in the morning. I get interrupted as I go to pray. And then, you just seem so far off, and I walk around feeling bad—like, somehow, I've disappointed even *you.*

The enemy jumps right on that, echoing over and over again in my head what I'm *not.*

But right now, I'm intentionally tuning out the enemy, the inner me, or even that part of me that is trying to build a wall between you and me. I'm listening for your voice. As much as I'm tempted to get distracted, as bad as I think I've failed, and as much as I feel like I don't measure up, I know I have a promise from you.

You're more than aware of my shortcomings, my failures, and all my crazy junk. And you love me regardless. No matter how I feel, nothing can ever separate me from your love. Your. Love. Never. Fails. *Period.* Not up for discussion.

Thank you, God, for never giving up on me. I know I am loved by you!

God's Word

"For I am convinced [and continue to be convinced—beyond any doubt] that neither death nor life, nor angels, nor principalities, nor things present and threatening, nor things to come, nor powers, nor height, nor depth, nor any other created thing, will be able to separate us from the [unlimited] love of God, which is in Christ Jesus our Lord."
— Romans 8:38-39 AMP

"Praise the Lord! He is good.
God's love never fails."
— Psalm 136:1 CEV

"Love never fails [it never fades nor ends]. But as for prophecies, they will pass away; as for tongues, they will cease; as for the gift of special knowledge, it will pass away."
— 1 Corinthians 13:8 AMP

I WON'T HOLD BACK

Hi God. Sometimes when I start to ask you for stuff, I chicken out.

I feel like I might be bothering you with trivial things. After all, you probably have a lot more important things to do. You might look at my requests and think they were, well, dumb.

I feel like I should be deserving of what I ask for, so I don't ask because I know what I've done and what I feel like I deserve.

I guess I feel like some things I ask for are selfish. But, over and over, your Word tells me to ask you for things. You're my good Father, and you love it when I come to you in faith with my requests.

I know I've been holding back, but not anymore. Not today. Today I'm going to have audacious faith—bold faith! Believe-God-is-bigger-than-I-can-even-imagine faith.

I'm not going to wait. I'm going to boldly approach the throne of grace and *ask* for things I want or need. I'm going to treat you like the "exceedingly, abundantly above-all-I-can-ask-think-or-imagine God" you say you are.

- Instead of praying just to pass the test, I'll ask for an A!
- Instead of praying for a ticket to the event, I'll ask for front-row seats!
- Instead of praying for a promotion, I'll ask to run the whole company.
- Instead of praying for rent money, I'll ask to own my own house.

Today I'm not letting the enemy hold me back from pleasing you, and I will put my faith and hope in you on display.

I take you at your Word, and I ask you for whatever I want and need. I believe in you enough to ask for big things. I'm not going to be nervous or timid anymore.

Right now, God, I ask you for . . .

_____

_____

_____

_____

God's Word

"Don't worry about anything; instead, pray about everything. Tell God what you need, and thank him for all he has done."
— Philippians 4:6 NLT

"Let us then fearlessly and confidently and boldly draw near to the throne of grace (the throne of God's unmerited favor to us sinners), that we may receive mercy [for our failures] and find grace to help in good time for every need [appropriate help and well-timed help, coming just when we need it]."
— Hebrews 4:16 AMPC

"Now to Him who is able to [carry out His purpose and] do superabundantly more than all that we dare ask or think [infinitely beyond our greatest prayers, hopes, or dreams], according to His power that is at work within us, to Him be the glory in the church and in Christ Jesus throughout all generations forever and ever. Amen."
— Ephesians 3:20 AMP

I'M ALL WORKED UP

Hi God. I'd love to tell you that I am calm, cool, and collected when I get bad news, but I honestly seem to get stressed out and lose my cool instead.

You'd think that normal, run-of-the-mill, trying-to-drive-me-crazy stupidity would be something I wouldn't let get to me, but I do.

I get so worked up trying to handle things myself because I feel like I'm responsible. I think that it's my job to make everything happen and solve the world's problems—or at least solve *my* world's problems.

I have to admit: in those frustrating moments, I seem to grumble about the problem, vent about why it happened, and complain about why I'm stuck in the middle of it. But instead of all that unnecessary drama, I should be running straight to you first.

You're my heavenly Father, the One with all the answers. You're the very creator of my soul. You're my rock, my fortress, and my hiding place. You can handle it all and make me look good in the process.

What I really need is a whole lot *less* of me and a

whole lot *more* of you. You're the true center of the universe—not me! You could solve all the world's problems in an instant and not even flinch. You are the answer. When I ask for your direction, you don't hold back at all, and you generously give it to me.

Wisdom is totally what I need in those moments. When I ask you for what you already know, you never leave me in the dark.

Father, I confess that I haven't been asking you for your wisdom. It's a big relief to trust in you and know that you have me in the palm of your hand. I don't need to be so aggravated. I don't have to sweat the small stuff anymore!

"And your ears will hear a word behind you, saying, This is the way; walk in it, when you turn to the right hand and when you turn to the left."
— Isaiah 30:21 AMPC

"If any of you lacks wisdom, you should ask God, who gives generously to all without finding fault, and it will be given to you."
— James 1:5 NIV

"Casting the whole of your care [all your anxieties, all your worries, all your concerns, once and for all] on Him, for He cares for you affectionately and cares about you watchfully."
— 1 Peter 5:7 AMPC

WHEN I NEED
TO SAY NO

Hi God. I'm desperately overcommitted, super busy, and totally stressed out.

I know it's my fault. I just keep saying yes to people, even when I don't really want to do what they're asking me to do. Sometimes I think I just agree because I'm afraid of the repercussions of saying no to people. What if they don't like me anymore? Or what if I get left out of things in the future?

I have to start seeing the value of what a simple no does for me—for my peace, for my relationship with you, and for the future you've intended for me. No can be a great word. It can keep me from wasting my time and energy.

I was created to please you, not people. I can't be worried about what everyone else wants me to be and still become what *you*, my Father God, created me to be. You have been waiting for me to look to you for my next step.

When I have trouble saying no to people, I'll think

of it this way from now on: It's my opportunity to say yes to something better. It's my chance to say yes to you and what you have for me.

When I say no to opportunities that aren't best for me, I've positioned myself correctly—with time, money, and energy—to say yes to the blessings, situations, and good that you have waiting for me.

I say yes to you and your blessings, God!

God's Word

"For we speak as messengers approved by God to be entrusted with the Good News. Our purpose is to please God, not people. He alone examines the motives of our hearts."
— 1 Thessalonians 2:4 NLT

"As surely as God is trustworthy and faithful and means what He says, our speech and message to you have not been Yes [that might mean] No. For the Son of God, Christ Jesus (the Messiah), Who has been preached among you by us, by myself, Silvanus, and Timothy, was not Yes and No; but in Him it is [always the divine] Yes. For as many as are the promises of God, they all find their Yes [answer] in Him [Christ]. For this reason we also utter the Amen (so be it) to God through Him [in His Person and by His agency] to the glory of God."
— 2 Corinthians 1:18-20 AMPC

"And be not conformed to this world: but be ye transformed by the renewing of your mind, that ye may prove what is that good, and acceptable, and perfect, will of God."
— Romans 12:2 KJV

WHAT AM I LOOKING AT?

Hi God. It might look like I'm down for the count, but looks can be deceiving. That's why you tell me not to look at what's happening all around me. You tell me to look at *you*!

The enemy does his best to distract me and bring my failures, problems, and stress back to memory. The dumb devil does that to everybody.

- I can't look at the size of the giant coming at me, though. David didn't care, and he had the whole army depending on him.
- I can't look at the size of the mountain you are asking me to climb. Size didn't stop an 80-year-old Joshua.
- I won't look at the number of people trying to get me. Numbers didn't stop Moses at the Red Sea with a million people to save.

I can't look at the problem, the medical report,

the financial bottom line, or the haters at work or on Facebook. You tell me not to trust in what I can see because the "look" of the situation will deceive me.

Instead, when I'm afraid, my job is to look to you. The One who I put my hope and trust in—no matter what my circumstances look like—is you. You're my God. You're my Savior. You save me. It is what you do.

With you on my side, what can man do to me?

It doesn't matter who is coming at me. With you on my side, my enemies don't stand a chance. They will fall like David's giant, crumble like Joshua's mountain, and be swallowed up like the army chasing Moses.

When the situation looks bad, and I'm surrounded by, overwhelmed with, and *in the very presence* of enemies, I am actually in the midst of a marvelous opportunity for you to show up.

I might not have started this fight, but I know you, God, are going to finish it. Boom!

God's Word

"My God, my rock, in whom I take refuge,
my shield, and the horn of my salvation, my
stronghold and my refuge, my savior; you save
me from violence."
— 2 Samuel 22:3 ESV

"When I am afraid, I put my trust in you.
In God, whose word I praise—
in God I trust and am not afraid.
What can mere mortals do to me?"
— Psalm 56:3-4 NIV

"What then shall we say to [all] this? If God is
for us, who [can be] against us? [Who can be
our foe, if God is on our side?]"
— Romans 8:31 AMPC

A PEARL OF
GREAT PRICE

Hi God. I want to live the life you have for me, but sometimes it seems like it's out of my reach.

When I look at all the dumb things I keep doing over and over again, I wonder how I could ever earn your affection. But it's not about me, is it? It's all about you!

I love how you picked me, how you think good thoughts about me, and how you have a plan and purpose for my life. You're even in heaven praying for me—that's so cool! Jesus told a story about a merchant who found a "pearl of great price." The merchant gathered all his stuff together, sold everything, and *gave it all* just to buy that one thing.

Jesus gave it all for me. He gave up his very life for me because he thought I was worth it. He thought I was treasured—that I was that one thing so precious to him.

It overwhelms me that you love me that much. I can't

even wrap my mind around it. Your love is hard to grasp because it isn't natural—it's a spiritual, supernatural love. Your love isn't about earning and deserving; it's all about believing in you and receiving from you.

I didn't pick me. You picked me. When I have trouble believing in me, at the very least, I know I can always believe in you. If you love me, created me, and sent Jesus to *die* for me, then I can grab on to that. I can believe that you see something precious in me!

God's Word

"Again, the kingdom of heaven is like a merchant seeking beautiful pearls, who, when he had found one pearl of great price, went and sold all that he had and bought it."
— Matthew 13:46 NKJV

"For God so loved the world that He gave His only begotten Son, that whoever believes in Him should not perish but have everlasting life."
—John 3:16 NKJV

"You did not choose me, but I chose you and appointed you so that you might go and bear fruit—fruit that will last—and so that whatever you ask in my name the Father will give you."
—John 15:16 NIV

I GOTTA LOVE WHO?

Hi God. I can't believe you want me to love my enemies. I want to yell, "But you don't know what they did!" But, of course, you do. That's hard to swallow sometimes. You love the people who did me wrong. God, I mean *really wrong*. And I think they *meant* to hurt me.

How do I keep from telling the world how horrible they are? How do I keep my mouth shut and love them instead? This is so hard for me!

I have to remember that you're not a God who gives us what we deserve. You had to sit there and watch people beat, torture, spit on, and crucify your only son in the most gruesome way. And then, you forgave them all and loved them.

Wow, God. I have so far to go.

I need your help here. Father, help me to forgive. I'm not going to be able to do this on my own, but with you, all things are possible—even this. If anyone can change my heart, it's you. You help me do things I could have never even *dreamed* about on my own.

I can start by treating people how I want to be treated. I have definitely done things I regret in my life. I want forgiveness and love, and so does everyone else. God, help me to love people the way I want to be loved.

Today, Father, I ask you to help me forgive the people who have hurt me and love them, no matter what they have done. I put the impossible in your hands knowing that you make it possible. Help me also remember that it pleases you when I am dependent on you to change my heart.

Thank you, God, for loving me through this and giving me the strength to be more like you!

God's Word

"But I say to you, love your enemies, bless those who curse you, do good to those who hate you, and pray for those who spitefully use you and persecute you."
— Matthew 5:44 NKJV

"He does not treat us as our sins deserve or repay us according to our iniquities."
— Psalm 103:10 NIV

"And Jesus said, 'Father, forgive them, for they know not what they do.' And they cast lots to divide his garments."
— Luke 23:34 ESV

"So whatever you wish that others would do to you, do also to them, for this is the Law and the Prophets."
— Matthew 7:12 ESV

WHAT SHOULD
I DO?

Hi God. So many times I go after things without checking with you first.

I make decisions—sometimes big ones—and I "forget" to pray. I forget to ask you. Actually, sometimes it doesn't even *occur* to me to stop and ask you because I think, *I've got this.*

And I *do* have it . . . right until it goes south, and then I start wondering, *How did this happen?*

I don't know why it doesn't go off more quickly in my lightning-fast mind that the reason I'm caught in such a bad place is because I forgot to check with you! I just lean on what I know, and *go*.

That's not the system you put in place. You said I should acknowledge you in everything I do, stop what I'm up to, and pray about everything, even the small stuff. But I just don't sometimes. Ugh!

I'm not sure why I think I know better. From your eternal viewpoint, you know how everything turns out. Why *wouldn't* I ask you?

So right now, Father, I ask for your forgiveness for venturing out without your blessing. Forgive me for getting myself into tough situations you never wanted me in. I'll lean on your promise to guide me, teach me, and direct me in the way I need to go. Please God, show me what is right and reveal to me what is best.

What I should do? How I should respond? Should I pause, or should I expedite? I'm so excited to see what you have in store for me!

God's Word

"Trust in and rely confidently on the Lord with all your heart and do not rely on your own insight or understanding.
In all your ways know and acknowledge and recognize Him,
And He will make your paths straight and smooth [removing obstacles that block your way]."
— Proverbs 3:5-6 AMP

"I pray that the eyes of your heart may be enlightened in order that you may know the hope to which he has called you, the riches of his glorious inheritance in his holy people."
— Ephesians 1:18 NIV

"I will instruct you and teach you in the way you should go;
I will counsel you and watch over you."
— Psalm 32:8 NIV

• • ● ● ● • •

I'M FEELING MOODY

Hi God. When I'm in a bad mood, the last thing I want to hear is that somehow it's my fault or that I have some kind of control over what I'm feeling. I mean, usually I'm in a bad mood because somebody did me wrong. They did something to me, and it's not my fault!

Then I come face-to-face with the reality that what happened to me may be out of my hands, but how I react to it is in my control. *Grrr . . .*

I can let bad news ruin my day or not. It's my choice.

God, help me to realize I feel the way I feel because I think the way I think. My thoughts control my feelings—that's a fact. I can make the decision, right now, whether or not I'm going to be happy.

You say to catch each and every negative thought while it is running around in my head and make it bow to your power. So, what do I think about to change the way I feel? You say I should think about whatever is good—whatever is happy or lovely or whatever I can be thankful for.

What is there that I can be thankful for?

It might take me a minute to look past the obvious aggravations that make me grit my teeth. *But* I have teeth to grit. And I have food to eat with those teeth. And I had money to buy that food. These are things I can be thankful for. These are things that can change my mood.

Thank you, God, for the parts of my body I don't even think about because they work just fine. I don't *have* to think about them! Thank you that I have access to food and somewhere safe to sleep. Thank you for my job and the provision you give me to buy the necessities.

I'm alive and got to live today. I'm a child of the Most High God, and that has its benefits. Father, forgive me. I can't be in too bad of a mood when I remind myself whose I am, who I am in you, and how much you love me.

God's Word

"For as he thinks within himself, so he is . . ."
— Proverbs 23:7 NASB

"Casting down arguments and every high thing
that exalts itself against the knowledge of God,
bringing every thought into captivity to the
obedience of Christ."
— 2 Corinthians 10:5 NKJV

"Finally, brothers and sisters, whatever is true,
whatever is noble, whatever is right, whatever is
pure, whatever is lovely, whatever is admirable—
if anything is excellent or praiseworthy—think
about such things."
— Philippians 4:8 NIV

DAMAGED GOODS

Hi God. Broken. Damaged. No good. *Worthless!* Why do all these words come rushing at me at different times?

Some days it feels like I hear every single one of these terrible words. But I don't hear them necessarily coming out of someone else's mouth. I hear them from inside my own head.

When I want to dream bigger than where I am today, it seems like a little devil is sitting on my shoulder telling me exactly why I can't do it. He brings up my past mistakes and things that have happened to me from so long ago. Somehow he tries to make these things hurt like they happened today.

I don't want to listen to him anymore. I just can't do it.

The enemy might be technically correct that I have a broken past, a damaged history, and some baggage. But the enemy is not right about my future.

You, God—you—make beautiful things out of broken people. You make a glorious future out of a fractured past. You have the most excellent way of choosing what the world calls "rejects" and making them *heroes*.

Murders, cheaters, thieves, adulterers, outsiders— these are the outcasts you chose to raise up in the Bible. Moses, David, and Paul were murderers. Arranging a murder wasn't David's only problem; he also slept with another man's wife. Paul was a self-righteous murderer of Christians. Noah was a drunk. Jacob was a cheater. Elijah was suicidal.

Imperfect people. Broken pasts. Damaged history.

Since I've never murdered anybody, these guys actually make me look pretty good! That must mean I have a chance. Hey, what do you know? That pesky voice on my shoulder shut up!

I didn't start my life; you did. I'm not alone in this. You're with me, and you've gone before me to help me finish, and finish strong. I'm not damaged goods. I'm a victory about to happen!

God's Word

"To all who mourn in Israel,
he will give a crown of beauty for ashes,
a joyous blessing instead of mourning,
festive praise instead of despair.
In their righteousness, they will be like great
oaks
that the LORD has planted for his own glory."
— Isaiah 61:3 NLT

"Then He who sat on the throne said, 'Behold,
I make all things new.' And He said to me,
'Write, for these words are true and faithful.'"
— Revelation 21:5 NKJV

"For we are God's [own] handiwork (His
workmanship), recreated in Christ Jesus, [born
anew] that we may do those good works which
God predestined (planned beforehand) for us
[taking paths which He prepared ahead of
time], that we should walk in them [living the
good life which He prearranged and made
ready for us to live]."
— Ephesians 2:10 AMPC

OBSTACLES OR OPPORTUNITIES?

Hi God. It seems like there are so many hurdles in my life: problems, difficulties, speed bumps—whatever. Father, I want life to be smooth and easy. I don't want obstacles at every turn.

It doesn't seem like you would intentionally put these stumbling stones in front of me. You aren't the God of obstacles. You are the God of opportunity, the God of possibility. With you, all things are possible. So why do I see so many roadblocks?

Maybe I'm not looking with eyes of faith. Things in the Spirit don't look the same in the natural. Where I see obstacles, you have for me opportunities—chances for something new and exciting.

Obstacles are opportunities, but they never look like that to me. Opportunities for what?

- Opportunities to receive more of your power
- Opportunities for you to get glory
- Opportunities to do things your way . . .

And your way leads to blessing.

You promise that no matter the situation, you'll make things work out for my good. So if good comes out of it, then it's an opportunity. Even if people are trying to lie about me, talk bad about me, or hate on me, you'll use that for my good and help other people too.

I'm sure Noah saw massive complications when he was trying to load lions and monkeys into the same boat. But really, you were saving his family and all of creation.

I bet Shadrach, Meshach, and Abednego had a problem with going into the fire. But you knew they would be safe, and it was an opportunity for your glory and for theirs.

When Peter stepped off the boat in the storm, he must have been shaking. But you had his hand. The obstacle was an opportunity for him to make history.

From now on, no matter what pops up, I'll try to see it for what it really is. I've been treating things like problems and backing off. But now, I'll seize them and celebrate the victory you have on the way.

It's not an obstacle—just an opportunity for me to shine in you!

"I don't think the way you think.
The way you work isn't the way I work."
— Isaiah 55:8 MSG

"But as for you, you meant evil against
me; but God meant it for good, in order to
bring it about as it is this day, to save
many people alive."
— Genesis 50:20 NKJV

"For our present troubles are small and won't
last very long. Yet they produce for us a glory
that vastly outweighs them and will last
forever! So we don't look at the troubles we can
see now; rather, we fix our gaze on things that
cannot be seen. For the things we see now will
soon be gone, but the things we cannot
see will last forever."
— 2 Corinthians 4:17-18 NLT

SHAME ON WHO?

Hi God. When my past creeps up and tries to drag me down because of what I've done, I know it's not you doing it. The enemy, and sometimes even the inner me, reminds me of certain things I've done and tries to anchor me in guilt and shame.

But, my past doesn't limit my future, and it doesn't define my future. My past doesn't even define *me*; it prepares me. My past is a place of reference—not a place of residency.

I might not be where I want to be, but I'm sure not where I used to be! I'm a work in progress.

You're the author and the finisher of my faith. You aren't done with me yet. You're still molding me. I'm still on the potter's wheel.

I know I'm forgiven, and I won't be pulled down by my past mistakes. Your love for me isn't based on my performance. Your love for me never runs out.

I don't have to be afraid anymore. You've freed me from the shame of my past mistakes and imperfections. You won't let me be humiliated. You help me forget what I've done and what has happened to me and replaced it with who I am in you!

You promise that instead of disgrace, I receive the inheritance you have for me—a double portion and happiness too! You're too good to me.

I know why I love you so much. It's because I can remember what my life was like without you. Look how far you've brought me, God. I don't ever want to go back!

God's Word

"Brothers, I do not consider that I have made it my own. But one thing I do: forgetting what lies behind and straining forward to what lies ahead, I press on toward the goal for the prize of the upward call of God in Christ Jesus."
— Philippians 3:13-14 ESV

"Looking unto Jesus, the author and finisher of our faith, who for the joy that was set before Him endured the cross, despising the shame, and has sat down at the right hand of the throne of God."
— Hebrews 12:2 NKJV

"Do not fear, for you will not be put to shame,
And do not feel humiliated or ashamed,
for you will not be disgraced.
For you will forget the shame of your youth,
And you will no longer remember the disgrace
of your widowhood."
— Isaiah 54:4 AMP

I CAN'T PLEASE EVERYONE, BUT I CAN PLEASE YOU

Hi God. I want people to be pleased with me. I want them to like me, to accept me. I want to be on the inside. I don't want to disappoint people, let them down, or be rejected. I don't want to be the "tag-along" or the one barely in the group.

It seems like I'm just chasing shadows when I run after the fleeting and fickle approval of humans. If I'm afraid of what people think, it can disable me. I'm finally figuring out this is true. I'm letting my happiness live in other people's minds, and that's no way to live.

Not even you can please everybody. People pray for different teams and different candidates. Some people don't even believe in you or like you! If everybody doesn't like the Most Holy God, how do I expect everybody to like *me*? It's a plan of the enemy to keep me spinning my wheels and getting nowhere.

I really can't control if people are happy with me

or not. I'm not supposed to please them anyway. I'm supposed to please you!

I've decided to turn my intentions toward pleasing you, not people:

- When I please you, you open doors of opportunity.
- My enemies can't stand against me. You actually make them at peace with me, when I please you,
- When I please you, your favor comes on me. You tell me, "Well done!"

You smile in my direction and fill me with purpose. You take me from where I am and give me the opportunity to do more, when I please you.

I can't live my life worried about what people want me to be and also be what you created me to be. Help me realize I don't have to be afraid of people, God. I just have to please you!

God's Word

"The fear of human opinion disables;
trusting in God protects you from that."
— Proverbs 29:25 MSG

"Am I now trying to win the favor and approval
of men, or of God? Or am I seeking to please
someone? If I were still trying to be popular with
men, I would not be a bond-servant of Christ."
— Galatians 1:10 AMP

"Whatever you do, work heartily, as for the
Lord and not for men."
— Colossians 3:23 ESV

"But just as we have been approved by God to
be entrusted with the gospel, so we speak, not
to please man, but to please God who
tests our hearts."
— 1 Thessalonians 2:4 ESV

DIVINE PROTECTION

Hi God. The world is flat crazy. I can't believe the violence and terrorism. How can people possibly be so mean and evil to one another?

When I watch the news and see stupid things happening—even in my city—it makes me nervous. Should I go out or travel?

Yes, I should. I *should* go out. I *should* travel. Because when I do, the people around me are actually safer because your presence goes with me. If people could see the security angels you have all around me, they would be whispering, "Who is that?"

"Oh, it's just me," I'd say. "Child of the Most High God!"

It doesn't matter what's going on in my office, in my city, or where I'm traveling. A thousand may fall at my side, but trouble won't come near me. You're my fortress. You're like a fortified, walled city around me. You can hide me—even out in the open—because your angels guard me in all my ways. I won't even hurt my foot on a rock. Now that's a security detail!

You give me the authority to declare the blood of Jesus, the hand of the Lord, and the protection of the angels:

- For each member of my family
- Over my workplace and my children's schools
- Over our vehicles and the routes we travel
- For my church family and pastors
- Over my home—from the top of the roof to the bottom of the basement—every window, every crack, and every door

Thank you, Father, for the authority and right to declare your divine security and protection money can't buy. I can relax knowing that when I listen and follow where you guide me, I am safe no matter where I am.

I don't ever have to be afraid because you have me covered!

God's Word

"So we may boldly say: 'The LORD is my helper; I will not fear. What can man do to me?'"
— Hebrews 13:6 NKJV

"No evil will conquer you;
no plague will come near your home.
For he will order his angels
to protect you wherever you go.
They will hold you up with their hands
so you won't even hurt your foot on a stone."
— Psalm 91:10-12 NLT

"The Lord is on my side; I will not fear.
What can man do to me?"
— Psalm 118:6 NASB

REST, NOT STRESS

Hi God. I'm all worked up. I remember not wanting to take a nap when I was little, but I didn't realize it would be this hard to find rest as an adult.

How do I forget all this junk in the middle of the night or in the moment when the bad news comes? I don't want to crave comfort food just to get me through the day. And I know having ibuprofen within an arm's reach isn't the answer.

You didn't create me to live anxious, upset, and freaked out. You don't want me tossing and turning instead of sleeping. You don't want me walking around under pressure with an upset stomach and feeling like a weight is on my shoulders. That isn't living in your promise. That stress is a curse.

You have redeemed me from the curse. In the name of Jesus, I'm going to turn the responsibility of everything to you. You want me to stop overestimating my power to fix the problem and stop underestimating you, so I surrender.

If I give my stress to you, you can do something

with it. Please help me quit picking it back up again and trust and believe in your rest. I have to rest in *you*. When I do that, you promise that you will take care of me.

God, you never sleep, so there's no sense in both of us being up. I think I'll get some rest!

God's Word

"Can any one of you by worrying add a single
hour to your life?"
— Matthew 6:27 NIV

"Casting all your care upon Him, for
He cares for you."
— 1 Peter 5:7 NKJV

"Come to me, all who labor and are heavy
laden, and I will give you rest."
— Matthew 11:28 ESV

"He gives power to the faint,
and to him who has no might he
increases strength.
Even youths shall faint and be weary,
and young men shall fall exhausted;
but they who wait for the LORD shall
renew their strength;
they shall mount up with wings like eagles;
they shall run and not be weary;
they shall walk and not faint."
— Isaiah 40:28-31 ESV

STRONG IN YOU

Hi God. When life comes at me a million miles an hour, I need strength. Please remind me that I don't have to be strong on my own. I *can't* be strong on my own. I need you.

I'm so glad you're there for me. I can always count on you to give me strength—strength that is bigger than I am. Strength that comes only from you.

Your strength in me isn't revealed in what I can do. It comes from overcoming the things I thought I *couldn't* do. You can do all things, so I can be strong in you and in the power of *your* might.

Lord. In you . . .

- I can find that perfect job.
- I can get over these hurt feelings.
- I'll face the bad diagnosis.
- I can deal with these crumbling finances.
- I will beat this horrible addiction.

In Jesus' name, I can do all these things and more.

I don't have to be strong on my own, and I wasn't even designed to be. I was designed to be strong in you. You are my strength. You are my fortress. In you I will trust. No plague, no recession, no problem, no depression, no terror shall come to my family or to me.

You make me strong, God. You make me brave. You make me courageous. You make me able. You make me mighty. You make me victorious!

I ask for your strength, right *now*, and I believe I receive it when I pray. I am strong in you, God!

God's Word

"In conclusion, be strong in the Lord [draw your strength from Him and be empowered through your union with Him] and in the power of His [boundless] might."
— Ephesians 6:10 AMP

"The LORD is my rock, my fortress
and my deliverer;
my God is my rock, in whom I take refuge,
my shield and the horn of my salvation, my
stronghold."
— Psalm 18:2 NIV

"But the Lord is faithful, and he will strengthen you and protect you from the evil one."
— 2 Thessalonians 3:3 NIV

"Have I not commanded you? Be strong and courageous. Do not be afraid; do not be discouraged, for the Lord your God will be with you wherever you go."
— Joshua 1:9 NIV

CONTAGIOUS THANKFULNESS

Hi God. If thankfulness is the hinge that the door of opportunity swings on, I think I've figured out why so many doors have been closed lately.

I don't mean to be negative, and I don't mean to complain. There is a lot of good in my life, but somehow my eyes keep shifting to the negative.

The Israelites struggled to enter their promised land because they couldn't stop complaining. I don't want that to happen to me. I can't be hateful and grateful at the same time. I choose grateful. I choose entering the promise as quickly as possible!

Your Word says I have to put on the garments of praise. If I can put on a smile for that stranger in the store, I can surely put on some thankfulness for the God of heaven and earth!

The funny thing about "putting on" is that it eventually becomes authentic—like a laugh. I can fake laugh for a minute, but something about it becomes contagious. Before long, I'm *really* laughing!

I need to get myself into contagious thankful thinking. You tell me to thank you for everything, and why wouldn't I? You give me literally everything, whether I deserve it or not.

God, I thank you because there's blessing in my life even in areas I sometimes gripe about.

- I moan about my busy schedule, but it means I have things to do.
- I protest about the housework, but it means I have somewhere to live.
- I whine about a far parking spot, but it means I have well-able legs to walk.
- I grumble about my crabby boss, but it means I have a job to pay bills.
- I nit-pick at my spouse, but you gave me someone to love me.

I ask for your forgiveness for complaining about the very things you've blessed me with. I choose contagious thankfulness that brings the promise!

God's Word

"Blessed are those that learn to acclaim you, who walk in the light of your presence, Lord."
— Psalm 89:15 NIV

"Rejoice always, pray without ceasing, in everything give thanks."
— 1 Thessalonians 5:16-17 NKJV

"Giving thanks always and for everything to God the Father in the name of our Lord Jesus Christ."
— Ephesians 5:20 ESV

IN THE FIGHT

Hi God. I'm tired.

I feel like I have been fighting and fighting, and I keep waiting for the bell to ring that tells me the fight is over. But it hasn't rung yet. I'm starting to wonder whether I have enough in me to make it or not.

Then I realize I'm thinking wrong.

I'm thinking that *I* have to make strength happen—like it depends on me alone. I don't really need any more strength, though. I need the God of strength!

You are the everlasting God. You never sleep. You never need rest. You never need a nap. You never need to recharge. You are charged up—full of life and ready to give it away when I need it. You give power to the faint. Wow! You're offering me *power*. I need power, and I'm connected to the God who has it.

You promise strength to the weary. Guess what? I qualify! You promise I'll walk and not get tired—that I'll run and not faint. You give me the strength and endurance I need to win this race, so I will wait on you.

When I wait on you, you renew my strength. I go

from red battery to full green and from an empty tank to full and overflowing—plus reserves! Thank you, God, that you're full of life and ready to give your life away when I need it.

I'll fight the good fight of faith, but not alone. It's not just me in the ring—it's you and me. The battle is yours, and the victory is mine!

Thank you, God, for being in my corner.

God's Word

"For the Lord your God is the one who goes with you to fight for you against your enemies to give you victory."
— Deuteronomy 20:4 NIV

"He gives power to the weak,
And to those who have no might
He increases strength.
Even the youths shall faint and be weary,
And the young men shall utterly fall,
But those who wait on the Lord
Shall renew their strength;
They shall mount up with wings like eagles,
They shall run and not be weary,
They shall walk and not faint."
— Isaiah 40:29-31 NKJV

"Fight the good fight of the faith [in the conflict with evil]; take hold of the eternal life to which you were called, and [for which] you made the good confession [of faith] in the presence of many witnesses."
— 1 Timothy 6:12 AMP

TAKE TODAY BACK

Hi God. Right until this second I was really thinking that today was . . . challenging. It's been like a day I don't want to live over again. These feelings, these emotions, try to take control of my mind and ruin the opportunities you put in front of me today.

I only get one chance to live this day, and it's a gift I'll never have again. The enemy tries to take it, but I have a choice. I can let the enemy take away something I can't replace, or I can take it back.

I choose to take today back.

I know I've had legitimate frustrations and reasons to be hurt or angry. But I can either spend time defending those feelings and getting stuck in those emotions, or I can lift them up to you and put my faith in you to turn it around.

I won't be controlled by my emotions or my situation. I have faith in you. I don't have to fall apart, be mad, and let my day be wrecked by feelings and circumstances. The enemy didn't make today. You did!

This is the day *the Lord* has made. You made today

for me to enjoy. You didn't make it to defeat me. You made this day with an opportunity for me to lean into you, trust you, and follow you.

The Bible gives clear instructions about what to do: Rejoice and be glad *today*. Bless the Lord, soul, and quit forgetting about the good stuff!

Today may have started bad, but it's rapidly on its way to becoming a great day only you can give.

In Jesus name, I'm taking today back!

God's Word

"The thief comes only to steal and kill and
destroy. I came that they may have life
and have it abundantly."
— John 10:10 ESV

"This [day in which God has saved me] is the
day which the Lord has made; Let us
rejoice and be glad in it."
— Psalm 118:24 AMP

"Bless the Lord, O my soul;
And all that is within me, bless His holy name!
Bless the Lord, O my soul,
And forget not all His benefits."
— Psalm 103:1-2 NKJV

I'M IN TROUBLE

Hi God. You're not going to believe what's going on. I almost don't believe it myself. I'm confused. I'm in trouble, and I'm scared. I need help. God, today I need one of your miracles!

Thoughts come to my mind that because of what I've done you might not be able to help me . . . or even want to. I'm not sure why you would want to help someone who's done some of the things I've done. But that's why I'm so thankful for your promises. They are there for me even when I don't deserve them. And they are a lifeline to me right now. You feel like my only hope. Hope. I need that right now—desperately!

You've seen problems bigger than mine and handled them. Mountains aren't crumbling down on my head, even though it feels kind of like that at the moment. You are a mountain mover, a sea suppressor, a light and peace giver, a faithful forgiver, and a miracle-working God! You're a giver of hope, a supplier of life, and an ever-present help in trouble. If I was in this alone, I would fall apart. But I'm not. You are in this with me.

You were in the lion's den with Daniel.

You were in the fish with Jonah.

And you are in the middle of this with me.

You never leave me. You knew this was coming. It surprised me, but it didn't surprise you. You're ready for this. As a matter of fact, you've gone through this before I was even here. You go out into my future and make a way for me to escape.

You promised that if I'd seek you, you'd answer me and deliver me from my fears. Here I am, God! I'm seeking you. I'm believing in you. I'm trusting you.

You have a plan and are at work behind the scenes where I can't see. You are full of grace and mercy. I am coming through this with you on my side—in Jesus' name!

God's Word

"God is our refuge and strength,
A very present help in trouble.
Therefore we will not fear,
Even though the earth be removed,
And though the mountains be carried into the
midst of the sea."
— Psalm 46:1-2 NKJV

"This poor man cried, and the
LORD heard him
and saved him out of all his troubles."
— Psalm 34:6 ESV

"I sought the Lord, and He heard me,
and delivered me from all my fears."
— Psalm 34:4 NKJV

"Be strong and of good courage, do not fear
nor be afraid of them; for the Lord your God,
He is the One who goes with you. He will not
leave you nor forsake you."
— Deuteronomy 31:6 NKJV

WHEN LIFE THROWS ME LEMONS

Hi God. I feel like I want to give up and give in, but I *hate* to lose.

I feel like I've lost steam, and yet, I'd like to be strong and push through this. Right now, I can't see how I can possibly win. I really can't afford to lose on this.

I know I can't win on my own. But with you, God, *all things are possible*. When my faith seems weak, and it looks like I'm going down, I know I can always count on you.

You promise to give me victory, and you never go back on your word!

- If there is a weapon that shows up in my way, you break it.
- Even though someone or something tries to push me down, you make a way for me to be on top again.
- If someone tries to become my enemy, you scatter their thoughts, their efforts, and even them.

- When life turns sour, you promise to work it out for me every time.

And just because I can't see you working doesn't mean you aren't. You're talking to people, moving things, getting opportunities lined up, and working in me to get me ready to break through.

Things aren't falling apart for me; they're falling into place!

Regardless of what things look like, I close my physical eyes now and begin to see with my eyes of faith. With faith-filled, trusting eyes, I begin to see my victory. Whatever dares defy my God doesn't have a chance. You cause anything that comes my way to work out for my benefit.

If life throws me lemons, you make lemonade. I'll sip on that!

God's Word

"So we fix our eyes not on what is seen, but on what is unseen, since what is seen is temporary, but what is unseen is eternal."
— 2 Corinthians 4:18 NIV

"But thanks be to God, who gives us the victory through our Lord Jesus Christ."
— 1 Corinthians 15:57 ESV

"Yet in all these things we are more than conquerors through Him who loved us."
— Romans 8:37 NKJV

"You intended to harm me, but God intended it for good to accomplish what is now being done, the saving of many lives."
— Genesis 50:20 NIV

• • ● ● ● • •

I'M GETTING ANTSY

Hi God. Life is moving at a crazy speed. Everybody is in a hurry. In the checkout line, people are griping because they have to wait. (OK, maybe it was me, too.) People won't even let a car merge into their lane of traffic. Why? Does it slow us down that much?

Microwave instead of oven. Fast food instead of real food. Don't wait—buy now! Call-ahead order. There's an app for that. Self-checkout (because, of course, I can do it faster than someone who is trained to do it . . . NOT!). We want a fast track with a speed pass to go, go, go!

And then, you are a God who wants us to wait. *Wait?* Why wait?

You're asking me to do things the whole world has me trained *not* to do. Wait. Have faith. Focus on you. Be patient. I feel like patience should be a four-letter word. No one wants to hear that!

- Let patience have her perfect work. *Couldn't patience work faster?*

- Be still and know that I am God. *Can't I do that on my way to work?*
- Those who wait upon the Lord shall renew their strength. *I do need more strength . . .*
- You act on behalf of those who wait for you. *Please act for me.*
- Waiting on you brings blessing. *Man, I need your blessing.*
- The Lord is good to those who wait for him. *I want your goodness!*

When I get antsy and want to hurry things along, I have to remind myself why I need to wait. Waiting for you, instead of trying to make *something* happen right now on my own, shows faith. And doing things your way always works out better than any of my crazy ideas anyway. Besides, I can't make miracles happen on my own. Through faith and patience, I get your promise. When I wait on you, the benefits are bizarre, supernatural, and beyond natural comprehension. They are unachievable by me alone, but do-able all day, *every* day by you!

You want me to wait on you. I can't imagine why I wouldn't. Every time I get antsy and want to move on my own to hurry things along, I'll remind myself of why I need to wait on you.

Thank you for being so good to me!

God's Word

"Wait for the LORD;
be strong, and let your heart take courage;
wait for the LORD!"
— Psalm 27:14 ESV

"But let patience have her perfect work, that ye
may be perfect and entire, wanting nothing."
— James 1:4 KJV

"From of old no one has heard
or perceived by the ear,
no eye has seen a God besides you,
who acts for those who wait for him."
— Isaiah 64:4 ESV

"The Lord is good to those who wait for Him,
To the soul who seeks Him."
— Lamentations 3:25 NKJV

I DON'T KNOW WHAT TO DO

Hi God. I feel like I'm surrounded by darkness. I don't know what to do. I'm sure it's no surprise to you because you didn't create me to know everything. If I did, I wouldn't need you.

You want me to come directly to you for answers, and you have the answers I need.

- You know how the universe is held together.
- You know how the body heals itself of a cut.
- You know just how far the ocean tides can go.
- You know exactly what to do when I have no clue.

Your Word lights up my path. You illuminate each step on the path in front of me as I get there, not before. That way, it's a step of faith. As I step out, you provide light.

I'm not afraid of the unknown because I know the One who knows all. I come to you for direction. I ask you for wisdom, and you gladly tell me.

It's your job to know what to do. It's my job to ask. I can do that!

The Bible says I have an anointing from the Holy One, and I know all things. I might not know it in my mind, but I know it in my spirit because that's where you illuminate the answers in me.

When the time comes, I'm confident I will know exactly what to do. I will do the ordinary, and I'll let you do the extraordinary!

God's Word

"Your word is a lamp to my feet
And a light to my path."
— Psalm 119:105 NKJV

"When His lamp shone upon my head,
And when by His light I walked
through darkness."
—Job 29:3 NKJV

"For everyone who asks receives, and he who
seeks finds, and to him who
knocks it will be opened."
— Matthew 7:8 NKJV

"But you have an anointing from the Holy
One, and you know all things."
— 1 John 2:20 NKJV

IN-CHRISTED

Hi God. Sometimes I feel like I'm not enough. It seems like everyone needs a piece of me, and I come up short. I feel like I'm not smart enough, fast enough, good-looking enough, funny enough, likable enough, talented enough . . . just *not enough*.

I get so into where I fail—my sin, what I've done—that I let it drag me down. I have this constant fear of not being able to live up to other people's expectations, especially when I look at who I am.

But you tell me not to look at who I am alone. You tell me to look at who I am *in Christ*. I'm in Christ. This is something I need to grasp. *You can't see me without seeing me in Jesus.*

I am not who I *think* I am. I am who *you say* I am. You say:

- I am a child of the Most High God, fully accepted by the Father. I don't have to worry about acceptance—I am accepted.
- I am fearfully and wonderfully made. Even

when I don't feel wonderful, I *am* wonderful because you say so.

- I am created for good. If I was created for good, I must be good.
- I am your masterpiece. No matter what I don't like about myself, you must have thought I was beautiful.
- I am not broken. I am complete in you.
- I am the apple of your eye. You love me beyond my comprehension.
- I am worth more than I think I am. I am valuable. After all, you sent Jesus to die for me.
- I am created for a purpose and a destiny, and I am equipped to live that out.

I've been "in-Christed." You encapsulate me. And when I'm in you, I'm new. Nothing like me has ever been before. I am a "me" I could never be on my own—a God-empowered, Christ-inspired me.

"Therefore, if anyone is in Christ, he is a new creature; the old things passed away; behold, new things have come."
— 2 Corinthians 5:17 NASB

"Put on your new nature, and be renewed as you learn to know your Creator and become like him. In this new life, it doesn't matter if you are a Jew or a Gentile, circumcised or uncircumcised, barbaric, uncivilized, slave, or free. Christ is all that matters, and he lives in all of us."
— Colossians 3:10-11 NLT

"And you are complete in Him, who is the head of all principality and power."
— Colossians 2:10 NKJV

IN NEED OF
WISDOM

Hi God. My view is limited in this world I live in. I feel like I'm trying to see something just out of sight. It's fuzzy to me. Sometimes I even think I know what I'm seeing, but really, I don't. Appearances can be so deceiving.

But you see the beginning to the end. You know where the traps are. You can see every misstep. You know which way brings blessing and which way brings danger for me.

What's amazing is that you're willing to share that wisdom with me! All you want me to do is ask you, and you promise to give me all the wisdom I need— abundant wisdom. Regardless of my faults, you still give me your wisdom.

So I ask for your wisdom right now, Lord. Please lead and guide me in the direction I should go. Speak to me. I'm leaning in. I'm listening. My ears are open. I want to make the right decision at the right time.

Your Word says that I'll be led with peace, so I'm

taking each step and then looking for peace. My heart and ears are open to anything you want to speak to me, even if I am afraid of what it will be. I trust you.

Your wisdom in me will open doors, make a way for opportunities, and take me places I never could have gotten to on my own.

Thank you, God, for your wisdom!

God's Word

"Wisdom is the principal thing;
Therefore get wisdom.
And in all your getting, get understanding."
— Proverbs 4:7 NKJV

"If any of you lacks wisdom, he should ask
God, who gives generously to all without find-
ing fault, and it will be given to him."
— James 1:5 NIV

"I will instruct you and teach you in the way
you should go;
I will guide you with My eye."
— Psalm 32:8 NKJV

WILLING, NOT WORTHY

Hi God. When I hear about the crazy amazing things your Word promises to do for me, I get excited . . . until I start thinking about me. I mean, I could never be good enough to be the person you pick to bless . . . could I?

You've seen everything I've done, so you know what I'm not. You know how I've messed up. I look around and see other people who seem so much more together than I am.

But, if I look at history, it's kind of funny how you never really picked those perfect people to use.

- Rahab was a prostitute, and you still picked her to save the Israelites and be King David's great-grandmother. She was in the bloodline of Jesus!
- Peter cut off a guard's ear during Jesus' arrest and denied Christ three times. But you chose him to be "the rock" on which the church was built.

- You picked Sarah to be the mother of Isaac. She was a woman who encouraged her husband to sleep with a mistress and then hated that mistress and the child she bore.

You've picked a lot of imperfect people to use just because they were willing. I don't feel worthy enough to be used, chosen, called, healed, or blessed. But I sure am willing!

Because you have plans to bless and prosper me, I won't wait to be perfect. I won't stall until I can get it all together. I'm taking my life off "pause" today.

I'm willing to be used, God. Pick me!

God's Word

"If you are willing and obedient,
You shall eat the good of the land."
— Isaiah 1:19 NKJV

"But if it is by grace [God's unmerited favor],
it is no longer on the basis of works, otherwise
grace is no longer grace [it would not be a gift
but a reward for works]."
— Romans 11:6 AMP

"For it is by grace you have been saved,
through faith—and this is not from yourselves,
it is the gift of God."
— Ephesians 2:8 NIV

WHEN GIANTS COME

Hi God. I wish you understood the size of what I'm up against.

I never imagined in my life that I would face something so hard. I never thought I would be up against this. I guess David never envisioned himself fighting a nine-foot giant in armor either, though.

But that was so long ago—it seems like a story, and this . . . *this*? This is *real*, God. It's happening now!

I'm trying my best to be strong, but I have this struggle between my head and my heart. I have these nagging thoughts telling me that the odds are against me. Time isn't on my side. What I'm praying for is just too much, too extreme, and too big.

But then there's my heart, and it keeps reminding me that nothing is too big for you. You're the God of the impossible!

When I read the Bible, I see that time after time you pick the little guy. You give victory to the underdog, the one who seems least likely to win. God, that seems like me right now. Then, when all is lost, and the situation seems hopeless, you step in and show yourself strong. You prove to the world that there really is a God in heaven!

I believe in you. I'm thankful for you. I'm going to trust in you so that I can find rest in you. You're my hiding place, and you're my strength. You're the one who makes the impossible possible!

Out of everyone on the planet, you chose me to be in this time and place. Thank you, Lord, for what you are about to do in my life. I have faith in you.

God's Word

"What then shall we say to these things? If
God is for us, who can be against us?"
— Romans 8:31 NKJV

"For with God nothing will be impossible."
— Luke 1:37 NKJV

"So be strong and courageous,
all you who put your hope in the LORD!"
— Psalm 31:24 NLT

NOT FINISHED YET

Hi God. I know you didn't create the world in a single day. But as you finished each individual day, you looked at the work completed and praised the progress made. Even though there was a lot yet to do, you looked at an unfinished work and still said, "It is good."

I'm definitely not finished yet. I'm a work in progress. Even though I know I have so far to go, I need to give myself a break. After all, I might not be where I *want* to be, but I'm sure not where I was when I started!

Can't I pause long enough to look at myself in my unfinished state and say, "It is good"? You've already done so much in me and for me!

Your hands are on me, Lord—continuing to form me and shape me as much as I will let you. As I make mistakes and become spoiled, you rework me into a vessel you can use. Mold me, God!

If you look at me as an unfinished work and *still* say I'm good, I should be able to give myself a little grace—not because I'm good, but because you made me, and *you* are good. As my good and perfect Father, you don't make anything that is junk—including me!

In this moment, I take permission to pause in the process and say for myself, "It is good." I am good. I am a product of my creator, and he is good.

You make beautiful things, God. You made me. And you're still molding me as much as I will allow you to.

You are the potter, and I am the clay. I am a masterpiece created in Christ Jesus. I am a work in progress. I'm not finished yet. Thank you, God, for continuing to work on me and in me.

God's Word

"But let patience have its perfect work, that you may be perfect and complete, lacking nothing."
— James 1:4 NKJV

"He has made everything beautiful in its time. Also, he has put eternity into man's heart, yet so that he cannot find out what God has done from the beginning to the end."
— Ecclesiastes 3:11 ESV

"Yet you, LORD, are our Father.
We are the clay, you are the potter;
we are all the work of your hand."
— Isaiah 64:8 NIV

"For we are God's masterpiece. He has created us anew in Christ Jesus, so we can do the good things he planned for us long ago."
— Ephesians 2:10 NLT